MW01287266

Analyze People

The Ultimate Guide to The Art of
Analyzing Human Behavior, Mastering
Body Language and Speed Reading
People on Sight

Leonard Moore

TABLE OF CONTENTS

Free Bonus:
3 Insanely Effective Words to Hypnotize Anyone in a Conversation

If you're trying to persuade and convince other people then words are the most important tool you absolutely have to master.

As humans we interact with words, we shape the way we think through words, we express ourselves through words. Words evoke feelings and have the ability to talk to the listener's subconscious.

In this free guide you'll discover 3 insanely effective words that you can easily use to start hypnotizing anyone in a conversation.

Go to **http://eepurl.com/cRTY5X** to download the free guide

Chapter One:
Human Behavior Basics Decoded

Countless realms of papers have been devoted to research about human behavior. Of course, it is at the base of driving all commerce, art, inventions, and relationships. It is at the core of comprehending how people act, decide, speak, memorize, and plan.

Why do you think people are investing in sensor technology and multi-modular data collection? Why do you think corporations are in a frenzy to study and analyze consumer behavior and psychology? There is a huge demand for research related to decoding the hidden secrets of the human mind.

Human behavior is a highly multidimensional and dynamic study field that requires various investigation points for offering accurate insights. You can't study one aspect of influencing human behavior in isolation to other factors. It is a complex web of several factors intertwining to form the fascinating whole.

Each factor contributes towards determining a majority of our behavior, though it varies according to the environment. Understanding human behavior is a complex task, and learning newer and more evolving trends in the science of human behavior makes it even trickier.

Why do people behave the way they do? What drives them to behave in a certain manner? What influences people's behavior and how can you use this knowledge for optimum benefit? What are the emotional hot buttons or motives behind people's behavior? Here are some of the most important points for decoding human behavior basics.

Classical Conditioning

Classical conditioning is a psychological process through which a human being learns behavior in pairs of stimulus and response. For instance, sour food generally stimulates salivation. The same process is in fact used in pet training, too. Each time your pet puppy fetches the ball, it gets a treat. Thus, it comes to associate a stimulus with a response, which means each time it fetches the ball, it knows the act will be followed by a treat.

Throughout our childhood, teen, and adult years, we experience this classical conditioning that molds our behavior. As a baby, we learn crying will get us our food. In our academic years, we learn studying hard gets us good grades.

The classic conditioning we receive throughout our life influences our behavior.

Today, it is used as one of the most powerful and widely used principles for understanding people's behavior.

Physiology and Human Behavior

There are certain and very specific physiological reactions to certain stimuli that help us analyze people. Yes, these are the very tools that are used in the arena of criminal investigations.

Using a series of biometric sensors, you can tell whether people are indeed behaving in sync with their thoughts or they are misleading/manipulating others. These psychophysiological techniques are powerful for deciphering the 'why's' that drive human behavior.

There are certain physiological reactions the human body undergoes when people don't speak the truth. It can be anything from dilation of pupils to increase in heart rate to twitching of toes.

People don't always display absolute honesty when it comes to voicing out how they feel. It may not always be due to the fact that they are manipulative or crafty.

Sometimes, it's more to do with their inability to express their emotions verbally or pressure to give a certain kind of response. It isn't always easy to coherently express your mood or emotions, is it?

Human Behavior and Emotions

An emotion is extremely scientific or clinical terms can be described as a short conscious experience comprising mental activity, and feelings that do not originate from a place of logic or knowledge.

For instance, even when we have pressing evidence of the fact that our partner has been unfaithful to us, we refuse to break ties. There is a tendency to act on brief impulses or feelings over reasoning and available knowledge (or evidence).

People's behaviors are primarily driven by their emotions. The ability to understand people's emotions gives us the power to understand or predict their behavioral patterns.

Human Behavior and the Subconscious Mind

There are three distinct layers a human mind is divided into – the conscious mind, the subconscious mind, and the unconscious mind. Consciousness is nothing but a state of awareness of our thoughts, actions, and experiences.

We are aware of everything we are feeling and perceiving. It allows us to process internal feelings, ideas, and thoughts that we accumulate from our environment.

However, a huge part of human behavior is driven by unconscious processes. Have you seen an iceberg? It has tons and tons of hidden or invisible layers. Our mind is pretty much the same. It has multiple layers, which even unknown to us, influence our behavior.

Like other biological creatures, we're perpetually reacting to our surroundings beyond our conscious mind.

Human Behavior and Experiences

While some psychologists ascribe a major portion of our behavior to genetics, others are of the opinion that our behavior is merely an aggregation of everything we've experienced since birth. They believe it is experience or the environment alone that shapes our behavior.

For instance, a person who is constantly differentiated against due or race or lack of privileged upbringing may turn out to abhor wealth or class. He or she will be likelier to empathize with the situation of the oppressed or underprivileged. Their life experiences have shaped their outlook and behavior.

Chapter Two:
Non-Verbal Signal Reading Secrets

Why do people insist on talking to someone about important matters in person rather than on the phone? Why are job interviews conducted in person, over simply sending across a resume and doing a phone call? It is without a doubt the need to read a person that drives us to have face to face conversations with them.

We want to analyze their expressions, gestures, posture, tone, physiological reactions, and more while speaking to them to give us a better understanding of how they are thinking and feeling. You do want to see your boss' expression when he compliments you about something, to know if it's genuine or he simply wants to get some additional work done from you.

Matching people's body language with what they are saying gives us a more well-rounded understanding of their feelings and personality, thus increasing our ability to read people's thoughts. Think about how it would boost your social proof if you understand exactly how people are feeling, and model your actions based on what they are looking for. Here are some of the best body language clues to gain comprehensive insights into a person's thoughts, behavior, and personality.

Nonverbal clues are a means through which messages are communicated between subconscious minds without the use of words. Verbal channels are not needed, and in effect, the message is determined by the medium. There are several nonverbal communication channels including facial expressions, body language, personal space, and the medium of touch.

Within multiple channels too, there is drastic variation. For example, facial expressions may not mean the same thing all the time. Similarly, not every expression is easy to decode. Research conducted in the area of expressions revealed that people are generally more adept at reading positive expressions such as happiness, excitement, enthusiasm, and positivity. This may be due to the fact that we are almost always looking for positive responses from others, and immediately detect it when we spot it.

Here are a bunch of valuable tips for reading body language like a boss.

1. You can be the ultimate body language master when you learn the more subtle nuances of reading a person's nonverbal clues, such as establishing a clear baseline for their behavior.

Let's just say that a person is hyperactive or restless by nature. They will constantly display signs of quick thinking and acting, such as fidgeting with their hands, prancing around from one place to another, and moving their legs. This may be interpreted as a sign of nervousness or worse deceit by someone who hasn't established a baseline for studying their behavior.

It is important to have a clear reference or baseline for someone's behavior to analyze them well in general. There will be instances, of course, where you will be meeting and analyzing people for the first time. However, by getting to know someone better personally make your insights even more powerful. It gives a more well-rounded and wholesome approach to the analysis process.

Let's consider an example. One of your close friends is a very fast-thinking, swift acting, and fidgety person. He is high on energy, and forever bouncing ideas off people. Someone who doesn't know this friend too well or doesn't have a baseline for judging him will inaccurately interpret his fidgeting as a sign of nervousness.

If you were to spot him on the street as a complete stranger, you'd believe he was nervous as hell. However, since you now have a clear baseline to understand he's hyperactive and excited about everything, you won't wrongly interpret his fidgety ways as nervousness. One of the biggest reasons why people misinterpret other's verbal and non-verbal signals is because they do not establish a clear baseline for people's behavior. The baseline acts as a foundation on which your entire reading or analysis is based.

Pay close attention to people's behavior all the time to understand their baseline. How do they behave and react in various settings? How is their speech and communication pattern in general? Are they in the habit of looking at people in the eye? Does their voice undergo a transformation when they're particularly nervous? How do they react when they are deeply interested in something? How do they communicate when they are preoccupied or disinterested in something? These are critical points when making an effort to read people. It eliminates all the potential fallacies you can make while analyzing people.

When you spot inconsistencies in their regular baseline behavior, it will be easier to tell something is amiss. It will help you keep an eye out for non-verbal communication patterns that are not in sync with their regular behavior.

2. Let's begin with the head. When people raise their eyebrows, they're most likely experiencing a sense of discomfort. Similarly, when they are lying or trying to hide something, their tiny facial muscles will start twitching. The eyes communicate plenty of the inner stuff you're feeling. When people maintain excessive eye contact, it can be a sign of aggression and intimidation. Similarly, a constantly shifting gaze can be a sign of deceit. One fallacy you need to guard against knowing the context and situation.

3. It isn't for nothing that the eyes are known to be the window to one's soul. They reveal almost everything a person feels or thinks without them being consciously aware of it. A constantly shifting gaze can be a huge sign of deceit or malicious intentions. People who don't look you in the eye while talking can seldom be trusted. There has to be a balance of eye contact. A shifting gaze can be a sign of nervousness and lying. Similarly, staring at a person for long can convey intimidation and aggression.

Similarly, when someone flashes a genuine smile, there is an unmistakable twinkle in their eyes. It can be a huge ice-breaker or sign that someone is happy to start a conversation with you. A twinkling eye and genuine smile can imply the person is friendly and inviting.

Blinking continuously is a huge sign of attraction. It reveals that the person blinking is enthralled or captivated at the person they are speaking to. Similarly, winking is seen to be a good-natured way to connect or flirt with people in Western countries. In the east though, it isn't seen as a positive act. Winking in eastern countries is viewed as a desperate and tacky way to approach a person of the opposite sex.

Research in the field of using psychology for analyzing people has revealed that a person who is engaged in a more stimulating conversation will have their eyes firmly fixated on the other person's face for about 80 percent of the interaction time. This doesn't mean the person should stare at you for 80 percent of the time. A more realistic pattern is – the person will look into your eyes for about a couple of minutes, followed by the nose and/or lips, and then quickly back to the eye contact. There is an occasional glance in another direction, but the gaze almost always returns to the eyes.

Can the direction of a person's gaze help determine their thoughts or feelings? When people look to their left, it is an indication that they are trying to recall something. Shifting their eye movements to the right implies that the person may be getting creative by misleading people and creating false versions of events. It can be a potential sign of deceit or manipulation. Please note that this is reversed in cases where the individual is left handed.

Direct and consistent eye contact is often a sign of high confidence, honesty, and courage. A person who constantly shifts his gaze comes across as mistrustful and deceitful. Similarly, excessive eye contact can be a sign of aggression, anger, and intimidation. If a person isn't looking away occasionally, they may be subconsciously threatening or intimidating you.

People who look back frequently while you are speaking may be disinterested or bored. They may either not be in agreement with what you are saying or impatient. It can also be a sign of preoccupation.

Eye contact is a huge sign of truthfulness. However, since most habitual liars are not adept at the art of lying and realize that a shifting gaze is almost always an indication of deceit, they will go out of the way to maintain unnaturally consistent eye contact. Watch out for clues to establish whether a person is being honest or deceitful.

Winking is seen as a sign of likeability and attraction. However, it isn't a favorable expression in all cultures. In eastern cultures, it is seen as offensive, rude, and disrespectful.

When a person looks up and then to the right while speaking to you, he or she is most likely disinterested or dismissive of what you've said. Dilated pupils, on the other hand, is a huge sign of attraction. It also means the person is highly interested or keenly listening to what you are saying. However, alcohol, LSD, and cocaine can also cause the pupils to dilate.

A smile that doesn't create crow's feet near the corner of the eyes isn't a genuine one. The sides of the person's eyes will be slightly crinkled when a real smile reaches their eyes. Smiles that simply move the mouth corners without affecting the skin near the eyes are nothing but polite, fake smiles that don't really show that the person is pleased about something. Rather, they are trying to appear pleased or forcing themselves to smile. It is virtually impossible to fake delight through a smile when you aren't feeling it. Look at awkward smiles in family portraits or photographs, where people are forced to smile by the photographer.

When people are anxious, their facial movements and blinking become more rapid. The mouth expands into a thin line.

Embarrassment can be revealed by quickly averting one's gaze, moving the head away, and offering a fake, nervous smile. If someone is constantly looking at the floor while they are speaking, they are probably upset or trying to conceal unpleasant emotions. Signs of anger, rage, or threat include wide eyes, open mouth (or upturned mouth expression), and a v-brow formation.

4. Speed reading a person is easy when you pay close attention to their upper limbs. Nervousness or boredom can be communicated by perpetually fidgeting with the hands. Crossing arms again is a huge sign of either anger or being totally unreceptive to what a person communicating.

If a person sitting across you is crossing their arms, they are subconsciously shutting themselves from what you are speaking. Get them to uncross their arms (and legs too) if you want them to listen to you with a more open and receptive mind. Arms placed akimbo can also be read as a sign of arrogance. Watch the way people are gesticulating with their hands. It will award you plenty of hints about the way a person feels or thinks.

Expansive hand movements can signify passion, energy, enthusiasm, and expressiveness. People also tend to use excessive hand movements when they are angry or upset. Notice how some people are constantly touching their nose or mouth? They are most likely ill at ease or even worse, lying.

Look at the context though before analyzing them. For all you know, they may be sweaty or itchy. Sometimes, people are plain fidgety by nature. This doesn't necessarily mean they are nervous or deceitful.

They may have a lot of energy, quick thinking, and have the need to constantly do something. This is exactly why it is important to establish an individual's baseline personality (what is their predominant personality in most situations), context and culture before jumping to spur of the moment conclusions.

Observing how people touch you can give you plenty of insights about their behavior and how they feel about you in general. Though touch is a tricky one since most people have their own idea about touches based on their personal bubble. However, like most body language cues, it can give you a good idea about what the other person is thinking or feeling.

A weak handshake, for instance, could indicate uncertainty, hostility, or nervousness. Similarly, the proximity of a person to you while you are speaking is a good indication of their interest in what you are saying or their feelings for you. People often distance themselves from others while talking when they don't wish to be intimate, affectionate, or vulnerable.

A research by the Income Center for Trade Shows reveals that if you shake hands with an individual, the chances of them remembering you double. People view you as being more friendly, warm, and welcoming when you shake hands with them.

While as a general guideline this is true, also take into consideration a person's baseline behavior. He/she may not be very comfortable being in close physical proximity to people, irrespective of the circumstances. Therefore, in such instances, a person maintaining a distance from you doesn't speak as much about you as it does about them.

Famous Hollywood talent scout/agent Irving Paul Lazar is famously quoted as saying that, "I have no contract with my clients. Just a handshake is enough." It speaks volumes about things you can judge about a person from their handshake.

Notice how people who are extremely demonstrative and expressive in nature talk through gestures, which offer a window to what they are thinking and feeling. Arms that are wide open indicate a feeling of being relaxed, at ease, flexible, and upbeat about novel ideas. These folks are not afraid to experiment with new ideas or enjoy new experiences.

Running fingers through the hair is a typical gesture of being uncertain or thinking what to speak next. The person is buying time to determine his or her subsequent move.

Similarly, rubbing the brow is a sign of anxiety or uncertainty. When a person covers their mouth while you are talking, they most likely do not believe what you are saying. Similarly, if a person uses this gesture while talking, it may not be wise to trust their words. It's a subconscious act where they are stopping themselves from speaking the truth.

If a person is stroking his or her chin, it may be a sign of deep thinking. Notice how people are constantly touching their earlobe during an interaction. It is a sign that he or she is seeking comfort since that is one of the body's most sensitive parts.

The palm up gesture is widely used to reveal openness and transparency. It is seen as non-threatening, friendly, and submissive. On the other hand, the palm down gesture can reveal power, dominance, authority, forcefulness, and aggression. Wasn't this Hitler's trademark salute?

Forming a steeple with both the hands may most likely indicate that the person is in a position of authority or self-confident by nature. It can also be used by people who want to show that they are in control or power.

Clenched hands reveal anxiety, frustration, stress, and restraint. Similarly, hands in the pocket gesture are formed when the person has a more closed attitude and wishes to keep to himself or herself. If it's only the left hand that's in the pocket, he/she is concealing something related to feelings and/or interpersonal relationships. We'll look at arm, hand, and palm movements in detail in another chapter.

5. When a person's neck and back are held high with a well-aligned posture, they are most likely confident and totally in control of their feelings. The shoulders are firm and do not lurch ahead. When the posture sags, it's most likely because they are subconsciously appealing to your sympathetic side and need help.

A constantly sagging posture can be a huge sign that the person doesn't boast high self-esteem. Keeping your posture straight albeit not stiff enough to look uncomfortable is a huge sign of feeling good in your skin.

Even the direction or position of a person's chin can reveal something about a person. For instance, a person who always juts out his or her chin is likely to be an obstinate individual.

Much of our body language is determined by our posture. The way we sit and stand reveals to a large extent what is going on inside us. Though the body language signals from the torso are more sublime, a trained eye can spot it without much effort.

An expansive and open torso posture is a sign of courage, confidence, assertiveness, and comfort. The person is comfortable in his skin or within the setting he or she is at.

A slouching position is a huge sign of timidity, submissiveness, exhaustion, or giving up. The person is subconsciously conveying his defensiveness.

Pay close attention to the way people react to your words and body language. Are they unknowingly mirroring or mimicking your actions? If yes, they are almost always comfortable, agreeable, and supportive of what you are saying. It begins with the posture. When a person starts mirroring your posture, it's a huge indicator of comfort.

6. Sitting in a cross-legged posture facing someone is an obvious sign of being close to what the person is saying. The person is not receptive to your ideas or treats them with disbelief. It is like a fortress around them that prevents people from accepting anything other than what they believe to be true.

Keeping your legs uncrossed is a huge sign of being open, comfortable, flexible, and relaxed. We can bring in the contextual element here too (more of that later). For instance, women wearing skirts or dresses will cross their legs not because they may not be open to what you are saying but simply because they don't want to reveal their thighs. If someone is uncomfortable with the way he or she is dressed, it will spill in their entire body language.

The situation will quickly deteriorate, and the rest of their body will appear awkward. They may not be nervous or anxious, they are plain uncomfortable with their clothes. Constantly shaking legs while being seated is a sign of nervousness, irritation, or boredom. The conversation or activity may not be stimulating enough to grab the person's attention.

Transferring weight from one leg to another can be an indicator of anxiety, nervousness, stress, disinterest, or discomfort. When a person is lying, he/she makes excessive foot movements to avoid stress or escape. Tapping feet is also a sign of nervousness or boredom.

7. Proxemics and Haptics is a sub-area of body language that is concerned with studying distance and touch to analyze an individual's personality. For instance, how close or away a person is standing from another person can reveal a lot about their personal equation or an individual's feelings for the other person.

We lean against a person or thing to lay our claim on it, much like declaring ownership over it. It is a subconscious, territorial way to show ownership. Notice how people lean against their vehicles or put their foot on it in pictures to reveal ownership.

When you lean against or touch a thing, you are indirectly conveying that is an extension of your body or something that belongs to you. Even lovers put their arms around each other to stake their ownership over each other and ward off potential competitors. Women will often dust away non-existent substance from a man's shoulder to demonstrate her claim over him.

Similarly, when people lean against things that belong to other people, it can be a sign of dominance, competition, or intimidation. People use proxemics and haptics to communicate the status of their personal relationships. Physical proximity and touch signals affection and a sense of ownership.

Likewise, when a person steps back while talking to someone, he or she is most likely not comfortable with the idea of getting too close to them. Looking at the distance between two people reveals a lot about their feelings for each other. Again, culture plays a huge role in studying proxemics. It can be subjective to cultures or vary from one culture to another.

For instance, in some liberal cultures, it may be alright even for strangers or new acquaintances to maintain a close distance while interacting. However, it may not be looked upon too favorably in more conservative cultures. Keep a person's origins in mind while studying them to get an accurate analysis.

8. Identify a group of clues as opposed to isolated ones. One of the biggest mistakes people make while analyzing body language is looking for standalone signs, without viewing a cluster of clues. It works wonderfully for slick poker player flicks but not in real life. One often has to view a group of signs or actions to come to a reasonable conclusion about a person's feeling or behavior. For instance, a person may be making eye contact, and you've been trained to believe that making eye contact is a sign of confidence, which means you ignore all other signs such as sweating, constantly touching one's face, etc. that reveal nervousness.

Always look for a cluster of clues rather than a single non-verbal clue. It is easier to manipulate a single clue than a bunch of everything else pointing to a clear thought or behavior pattern.

Spotting one cue shouldn't make you jump to an instant conclusion. For instance, a person may be leaning in the opposite direction from you not because they aren't interested, but simply because they are uncomfortable. If you are depending heavily on non-verbal clues, ensure that you spot at least three to four signs pointing to a clear thought process or behavior.

Try and take cues from different non-verbal communication sources. For instance, you may want to collectively analyze someone's tone, facial expressions, posture, hand gestures, etc. to be sure your analysis is accurate. Working in clusters increases your chances of reading an individual's behavior accurately.

9. The cultural context is crucial when reading body language. Though some body language cues like eye contact and smile are universal, many non-verbal clues have a clear cultural context or baseline. For example, Italian culture involves overtly expressive gestures such as plenty of waving, loud talking, excited voices, and shouting.

In Italian culture, excitement is more conspicuously expressed than say in the UK. The non-verbal communication pattern is much more upbeat and loud, which can make it hard for the Italians to interpret the behavior of someone coming from a predominantly British or American culture, where excitement is more subtly expressed. Therefore, viewing things in a cultural backdrop is important, especially if you're involved in doing business or forging political relationships with other cultures.

Even seemingly similar gestures can have an entirely different meaning in another culture. For example, while the thumbs-up sign (yes the same gesture through which we seek approval and validation on social media) is a symbol of validation in English speaking nations, it is considered inappropriate in some regions of the Middle East and Greece. Similarly, while making an "o" sign with your forefinger and thumb signifies OK in English-speaking nations, it is considered a clear threat in Arabic nations.

Personal space is almost sacred in Western corporate culture, so respecting associates and clients when they put up some barrier (like a bag or purse) is important. The amount of executives and managers who lose out on business deals for not interpreting these clues isn't even funny.

In addition to the cultural context, consider the overall context of the situation or circumstances under which the behavior occurs. Some settings (like a job interview) require a more formal behavior so sitting in a particular posture or gesticulating in a particular manner should not be misinterpreted. It can simply be attributed to the demands of the situation.

For instance, your body language at a pub when you are out with co-workers on Friday evenings varies considerably from your body language when you're with them at work. Non-verbal signals will vary according to the situation, so try to ensure that when you're analyzing people, you're also taking the situation into consideration. This will prevent you from wrongly reading a person who is spending a relaxed Friday night with co-workers as laidback, non-serious, and disinterested.

10. Reading body language on a date can be effortless with some practice and skill. Assume it is your first date with someone. Can you imagine how incredibly helpful body language can be in helping you gain insights about the person's behavior/personality, which can, in turn, determine if he/she is a good match for you? Obviously, it's not easy reading people on first dates. Everyone's trying to put their best foot forward. You're also trying to be as charismatic as possible, while also expressing your interest in listening to what the person is saying. Where is the scope for analysis here?

Pretty much like everything else in life, with a little practice and keen eye, you'll learn to spot the right signals effortlessly, without investing too much time.

It isn't rocket science or anything overly complicated. Just tune into simple things like how guarded they are with their body. Initially, everyone will appear guarded. They will most likely cross their legs or arms, and keep a fair physical distance from you. The palms will generally be held facing them. This is reasonable on a first date.

However, as an observer, you'll have to determine if it slowly transforms into a more open, warm, and welcoming during the course of the date as the comfort level between you and the other person increases considerably. By observing their body language, you'll quickly know if they are genuinely interested in what you are saying and that if they are naturally connecting with you by demonstrating a more open body language.

We have a tendency to mimic or mirror other people's behavior. So if you want the other person to look and feel more relaxed and less tensed, take on a more relaxed posture yourself. They will most likely mirror your actions and match your behavior.

Leave your arms uncrossed, give an honest smile, avoid physically distancing yourself from the date, and reveal your palms. These cues convey that you are warming up to the other person, which will also make him/her comfortable. Of course, the level of comfort will keep fluctuating during the course of the date, and it will be nerve-wracking to maintain a standard demeanor. If you observe that a particular topic is stimulating a particularly negative body language, stop in your tracks and change the subject quickly.

11. The tone of a person's voice. A person's tone can speak volumes about what he/she is thinking or feeling. If you observe several inconsistencies in the person's tone, they may be more excited, angry, stressed, or nervous than usual. It can also be an indication of hiding important information or lying. On the other hand, the volume of a person's voice while speaking can also be revealing. If they

are speaking in a tone that is softer and slower than usual, something may be amiss.

A person's tone can add several layers to the communication to make it more impactful, while also lending more meaning to what they are conveying. For instance, when a person says, "you are looking really nice today" in a sarcastic tone with emphasis on "today", you know they mean you don't usually look this nice every day and that they are surprised that you can actually look this good! Even though the person has offered you a compliment on the face of it, their tone and emphasis help you read between the lines.

The meaning of a sentence changes entirely when you change the tone or inflection. For example, if a person says, "She stole the ring" in a flat tone, he/she is making a statement accusing someone in a definitive manner. Similarly, if the tone is slightly raised towards the end, they are questioning or raising a doubt about the accusation. The words used are exactly the same but the intonation awards it an altogether different meaning. When someone speaks in a flat tone than raised tone often, they may have a more authoritative and assertive personality.

Emphasizing on different words can also alter the meaning of a sentence. For example, a sentence like, "Did you steal the book?" can have several different meanings when the emphasis changes. If the person emphasizes on the book, they may mean did you steal the book or something else. Similarly, if the emphasis is on you, it may imply did you do it or was it done by someone else. Again, emphasizing on steal would mean, did you steal it or simply borrow it with the intention of return it. There, emphasizing on three different words has given us three distinct meanings.

12. Consider the setting too. Sometimes the setting also influences a person's behavior. For instance, the same

person's body language will be different at work (more formal, restrained, and rigid) with co-workers than when he or she is socializing with them over the weekend (more casual, comfortable, gregarious, and flexible) over the weekend.

Similarly, a person who is otherwise confident and self-assured may show signs of nervousness during a job interview. It is the setting or situation that causes a shift in the person's behavior. For all you know, a person may cross their arms and legs because they are feeling cold or they may lean in the opposite direction because the seating isn't very comfortable. This is precisely why you should be looking at a cluster of signals rather than relying on a single clue.

Chapter Three:
Reading Expressions and Microexpressions

Facial expressions (including microexpressions) are one of the most foolproof nonverbal mediums of determining the thoughts and feelings of a person. Facial expressions are involuntary reactions that offer a sneak peek into a person's mind. Microexpressions are fairly reliable indicators of a variety of emotions that are subconsciously experienced by people.

What are Microexpressions?
A microexpression is a snappy, involuntary expression that is obvious on the face of a person in lieu of the emotions he or she is experiencing. Contrary to extended facial expressions, these are almost impossible to fake. What makes micro expressions so reliable is the fact that they occur as rapidly as 1/15 of a second. How does one fake something that happens so instantaneously and involuntarily? Microexpressions can be classified into seven primary emotions – anger, sadness, surprise, disgust, happiness, fear, and contempt.

Learning to decipher the meaning of a person's facial expressions and microexpressions gives you the superpower to unlock people's innermost emotions without them having to say a word about it. Research has proven that our facial expressions remain universal. Someone who has had an increased exposure to the media will demonstrate sadness or anger in much the way as indigenous tribes who have never been exposed to films or television. Even people who are born without eyesight display the same expressions as a person who isn't visually challenged.

To get good at reading people's expressions, start with yourself. Follow your own expressions by standing before a mirror. Watch what these expressions look like on you before you can start identifying them in others. You will realize that when you make a particular expression, you will actually start experiencing the emotion in what is called a reverse effect while studying body language. It isn't just emotions that lead to facial expressions but also expressions influencing emotions. Our faces are windows to our soul, if you master the art of reading it. You can tell a lot about a person simply by looking at their face.

Here are some tips to get you started with reading a person's facial expressions accurately.

1. Expressions such as happiness or delight are fairly easy to read. They are marked by a genuine smile. How do you tell a genuine smile from a fake one? The biggest sign is that a fake smile will never impact the eye muscles. It will at best be a polite or formal smile, not an authentic or genuine one.

When an individual is happy, their smile crinkles the skin to create crow feet on the skin and elevates their cheeks. The corners of your eyes crinkle slightly. It is widely believed that a smile can rarely be faked. The crow feet bundle up a little below the eyes to create wrinkles. This is exactly why people look so odd in photographs when they are faking smiles for the camera. It is nearly impossible to fake the crinkles and crow feet because that is only created when you are truly happy or delighted from within. You have to subconsciously experience happiness, enthusiasm, and delight to create this particular expression.

2. Let's talk about the angry face. Anger or aggression is easily noticeable on a person's face. Angry faces have eyebrows which are ever so slightly lowered and held together. Eyes stare hard or bulge to create vertical lines between the person's eyebrows. The lower eyelids become more withdrawn and tensed. Nostrils flare up, and the mouth becomes pressed together. The lips are more often than not drawn down in the corners or in a shape as if the person is shouting. The lower jaw is almost always jutting out.

3. Sadness is revealed by drawn in eyebrows. The skin under your eyebrows forms a triangle within the inner corner. The corners or ends of the lips are curved down. Pouting lower lips and raised jaws are an expression of anger. According to research conducted in the field of expressions, it has been concluded that sadness is the hardest to manipulate. You really can't fake being sad unless you are an exceptional actor, in which case you would've mastered the art of using your face for creating brilliant microexpressions.

4. How does one read fear on a person's face? A face that reveals fear has slightly elevated eyebrows that are flat and not arched. There are a few wrinkles on the forehead between the brows. The person's eyelids are slightly raised; however, the lower eyelids are tensed. The person's lips are generally tensed or withdrawn. The mouth is more open and the nostrils noticeably flared.

5. Pay close attention to a person's macro expressions that accompany specific feelings or emotions and goes on for 4-5 seconds. As opposed to microexpressions, macro expressions are revealed on the entire face. These expressions appear when we are all by ourselves or in the company of close friends and family members. Macro expressions are more extended than micro expressions because the person doesn't feel the desire to control it. They are relatively easy to spot if you know exactly what to look for.

6. Surprise is conveyed by eyebrows that are slightly raised and arched. The skin below the eyebrow is pulled and you'll spot horizontal wrinkles on the forehead. Eyelids stretch widely and reveal the whites under or above the pupil. The person's teeth will be parted, while the jaw appears dropped.

7. Inability to read facial expressions does not reveal what is causing the emotion. It only shows you that a person is experiencing a specific emotion or feeling. Don't start firing questions based on assumptions. Get to know more about what is causing the feeling by asking questions such as, "Do you want to say something about how you are feeling?" This is effective if the person is trying to hide his or her emotions.
Avoid asking people, especially if you share a more formal relationship with them, if they are feeling angry or upset. It may appear too intrusive, and you may end up upsetting the person even more. Spend some time developing a comfort level with the individual before they feel comfortable taking direct questions from you.

8. Cultural differences also come into play when it comes to reading a person's facial expressions. While it has been proven by multiple studies that facial expressions of basic emotions are universal, they can be interpreted differently by different cultures at times. According to research,

Asians rely more on eye expressions to understand a person's feelings and emotions. Similarly, Westerners are more dependent on the mouth and eyebrows when it comes to emoting. This may lead to misinterpretation of messages and faulty cross-cultural interaction.

9. Eye contact is a powerful tool for decoding a person's emotions. A trained people reader will quickly know a lot about a person's mood simply by looking into their eyes. Notice how a person's pupils dilate when they are stimulated or there is a change in lighting. A large pupil is a sign of interest, attraction, or arousal. When you a person's pupils enlarge on seeing you, you can almost always be certain that they are attracted to you (if there are no external environmental conditions).

Similarly, the pupils shrink when a person witnesses something shocking or offensive. People often squint when they don't agree with or appreciate what you are speaking. This is also a reaction when someone is particularly distrustful of your words or actions.

People who do not maintain consistent eye contact or dart their gaze in all directions tend to be insecure, untrustworthy, or comfortable. People who are comfortable looking into your eyes while speaking and shift their gaze occasionally are not just interested in what you are speaking but also more self-assured and trustworthy. By looking at you continuously, they are indirectly offering to let you peep into their thoughts and feelings, readily visible in their eyes.

These people aren't suspicious or uncomfortable about what you are speaking. Sideway glances also convey discomfort and insecurity. If a person is constantly breaking eye contact, they are only physically present. Their thoughts are almost always wandering elsewhere. Draw their attention back to you before you say anything further because they aren't really processing what you are speaking.

Excessive eye contact is also not very positive. It can indicate intimidation, threat, and aggression. If a person's eyes are firmly fixated on you, accompanied by a clenched jaw and lips, they are more often than not trying to scare you subconsciously.

10. No, this isn't about your nose growing a few inches long when you tell a lie. However, the nose is an easy part to analyze because it is located in the middle of your face. It is common knowledge that flared nostrils are a sign of anger or preparing for combat. People also express their displeasure through flared or bloated nostrils. Sometimes the nose will crinkle as a consequence of bad odor.

The above act also has metaphorical connotations. People crinkle their noses at the thought of something they don't find too pleasing or approve of. It is akin to scoffing at something or looking down upon an idea. Think of the idea as something the person doesn't approve of. At times, the nose's blood vessels will involuntarily dilate, thus revealing that the person is lying. The nose looks swollen and reddish. When we mockingly tell people that their nose will get red when they lie, there is actually a physiological process behind it.

11. Reading disgust is also fairly easy if you practice by observing people's expressions consistently. A disgusted person's face will have downcast eyebrows, however, the lower eyelid will be slightly elevated, thus making the eyes a tad too narrow. Their cheeks will be slightly raised. Similarly, the nose will be scrunched and the upper lip will be twisted or curled in an upward direction.

12. Lip movements are other dead giveaways of a person's feelings. Lip muscles are very fragile and hence are quickly

receptive to a variety of emotions. They reflect our moods, thoughts, and reactions to situations. Lips pointed inward are referred to as pursed lips, which is a sign of stress, frustration, mistrust, or disapproval. They are trying hard to control their emotions or literally biting their lips to prevent from speaking their heart out, which is causing stress. It is an expression of holding back feelings.

Again, puckering lips or pouting is a clear sign of desire. It can also convey boredom or uncertainty. Closely observe how people's lips will begin twitching when they are mistrustful or cynical about a person or idea. Liars can easily give themselves away if you quickly notice the slight twitch on their lips.

13. The eyebrows are one of the most important facial features to be studied while speed reading people's expressions. Despite the low number of attached muscles, the eyebrows are quite prominent and receptive to multiple emotional states. The forehead wrinkles in sync with the eyebrows. The expressions of the forehead almost always match that of the eyebrows, which makes for an impactful analysis.

When the forehead is wrinkled and the eyebrows are elevated, the person is raising doubts about your thoughts or behavior. They are suspicious of your motives. It can also be an expression of receiving the unexpected or being totally surprised by how events have unfolded. When their eyebrows are slightly lowered and the eyes are a wee bit hidden, the person is desperately trying to hide their feelings from you. They do not want you to see how they are feeling.

When a person's eyebrows slope inward or are more pulled down, it can be a sign of frustration, stress, or anger. The expression can also be that of intense focus. Sometimes, you'll notice a horseshoe style fold in between a person's eyebrows. This is an expression of grief or extreme unhappiness. The person just doesn't see a ray of hope in what is happening to them.

Chapter Four:
Reading Hand Movements

Reading arms and hands is one of the most effective giveaways for understanding an individual's thoughts, feelings, and emotions. Notice how animated people get when they are particularly happy or in an engaging conversation. They will move their hands in a more animated manner. People tend to use their arms and hands probably more than any other part of the body while speaking.

Just notice how children gesticulate while narrating an incident or story. It is a different game with adults because we've learned to hide our emotions through our body language. This limits our gestures and movements. However, the subconsciously guided process doesn't stop.

Watch an adult arguing or putting forth their point in a discussion passionately. When people are particularly angry or excited, their hand movements become conspicuously animated. Arm gesticulation is accompanied by emotions and more unrestrained, childlike gestures.

Even when people are more suppressed, their hand movements are unmistakable, especially for keen body language observers. Hand and arm activity aren't very challenging to read within the overall context. Here are some clues to unlock the secrets of the mind through your hand and arm movements.

Cultural Differences

Hand gestures can vary dramatically from culture to culture. For instance, in western countries, holding hands between heterosexual men are not considered appropriate. It is simply not the norm. However, in Arabic countries, it is seen as a sign of trust and confidence if a heterosexual man holds another man's hand.

Pulling your hand away in such a scenario can come across as extremely rude. Similarly, the thumbs up is seen as a gesture of a job well done or best wishes in western countries. However, in some cultures, it is viewed as a sign of rudeness or aggression.

Miming Hand Movements

Hand movements are used for conveying meanings and miming, which shouldn't really be confused with body language. Sometimes people self-mirror or gesticulate to demonstrate an act. For instance, someone may talk about pushing a car and gesticulate with his palms down. It shouldn't be read as a palm down gesture meaning the person is close to what you are saying. This is nothing more than a mime.

However, the manner in which people perform mimes can offer plenty of clues about their thoughts, feelings, and mindset. For instance, someone may gesticulate in a more sluggish manner indicating a lack of enthusiasm or openness to an idea. There are cultural differences to consider, too. For instance, people in the Mediterranean region are known to gesticulate more animatedly than folks from North Europe.

It has been noticed that people who have a limited vocabulary tend to utilize their hands and arms more often than people who are more linguistically eloquent. For all you know, you may be communicating with a person who isn't very verbally savvy. This will prevent you from misreading hand and arm clues.

Body language interpretation becomes more effective when you guard against these potential reading fallacies. Always bear in mind that you are looking for a cluster of clues and not isolated gestures. When you look for the complete picture and not stand alone signs, you increase your chances of making accurate speed readings.

When the Cover is Blown

When people are lying or tend to fear getting caught, their arm and hand movements suddenly become less prominent. However, again, this should also be read by establishing a baseline, context, and even cultural differences.

For example, if a person is otherwise animated and expressive while talking suddenly acts more restrained when posed with confrontational questions, they may simply be avoiding detection. This is because, on a subconscious level, they are thinking that less movement will decrease their chances of being given away. They are more guarded against being exposed or given away through their body language or movements.

The motive is to avoid being noticed. It is akin to a freeze response where say a shoplifter or suicide bomber will make their hands much less animated and inconspicuous.

People caught telling a lie or doing something wrong will freeze or stop arm/hand movements for some time to quickly avoid the topic and move on.

Palm Positions

Numerous studies indicate that palms up reveals positivity and openness to the idea. On the contrary, palms down can convey negativity, rigidity, and being completely closed to the idea being communicated. It can also convey neutrality of thought. Palms up are a fairly reliable indicator of honesty and transparency. Subconsciously, they are conveying that they have nothing to hide.

People who are trying to convince others about a product or idea tend to use a lot of palms up gestures to convince people that they are genuine and have revealed all details. Say, for example, you are planning to negotiate buying car, the salesman may maintain a palm up behavior to indicate that he won't lower the price any further. He believes he is being open and honest.

Observe where his palms are placed. If they are placed on the table, he may be more firm or emphatic in his decision. If it is just a palm up gesture, you can try negotiating further because they are only trying to give you the impression when they are not. However, palms on the table can mean they aren't willing to relent any further. Now, body language isn't always as straightforward as that. Things are not very obvious immediately. It is for the reader to analyze the finer nuances of gestures by putting it in the right perspective.

There's a popularly held belief that people who don't usually gesticulate while speaking are less trustworthy. Politicians, criminals, and habitual liars know this fact very well, which means they use a lot of hand or arm gestures to indicate honesty. People who are in more authoritative positions and don't want to appear rude often tend to keep their hands straight and avoid pointing.

Handshakes

Handshakes are one of the most prominent indicators of a person's aura and personality. There's a lot written about the importance of handshakes in communication. People who have firm handshakes (firm though not the type that completely crushes your hand, in which case it would be intimidation or aggression) and smile while shaking your hands are self-assured, confident, and positive about the meeting.

Similarly, a limp handshake indicates lack of confidence, disinterest, low self-esteem, or even a hand injury (there we can never ever make foolproof assumptions without knowing the context or looking for a cluster of clues).

A firm grip can also be too contrived since people now know the importance of a firm handshake. It is easy to fake an assertive handshake but look for other clues that can be clear giveaways.

Finger Pointing

Pointing a finger at anyone while communicating is a gesture of power. People often point their fingers while addressing an audience to impose their ideas or themselves on their audience. Parents point a finger while talking to their children to signify authority. It is mostly viewing at looking down upon someone or a sign of anger/ aggression. It can also be a sign of arrogance, confrontation, conflict, and offense. Jabbing a finger at a person takes this aggression to the next level.

The act of pointing fingers is not considered appropriate or polite. It has more negative connotations than positive.

However, a playful finger and wink are considered a more positive expression of acknowledgment or validation.

Similarly, jabbing a finger in the air while speaking is emphasizing on what the person is saying. It helps the audience develop conviction and confidence in what the speaker is saying. You'll often notice politicians, global leaders, and religious preachers pointing their finger while addressing their audience.

Clenched Hands

Research has indicated that hands clenched together are a huge sign of frustration, implying that the person is trying hard to curb a negative attitude. Take some quick action to subconsciously make the person more relaxed and open. This will unlock the person's thought patterns and make them more open to the idea you are presenting.

What happens is that it isn't just our subconscious thoughts impacting our actions or behavior. The reverse is also true. When a person changes his body language, he or she sends an involuntarily message to the subconscious mind. The mind then directs subsequent actions in the direction of the message it has received from the body.

So, while your actions are influenced by subconscious thoughts and feelings, the thoughts can also be altered by bringing small changes in the body language. When you get a person to sit or stand in a particular manner, their thought process can be manipulated to your advantage.

Gestures such as pointing at others can signify dominance. It can be a way for people to subconsciously communicate their status to others. Similarly, dominant people will have a firm handshake with their palm facing down. The grip is firm, sustained and demonstrates absolute control.

Disagreement

There are many arms and hand movements that are fairly accurate indications of disagreement, dislike, or disinterest. When people aren't very receptive to ideas or dislike something they hear, they subconsciously pull their hands near their body. It's akin to withdrawing into a shell or recoiling on hearing something that isn't particularly pleasing or agreeable to them.

This also happens because the person is subconsciously trying to reassure themselves with a self-hug. It is a sign of stress, disagreement, and mental conflict.

Steepling Hands

People who are confident, self-assured, and in authoritative positions often keep their hands in a steepling position. They are conveying a confident attitude to other people. This gesture is often used when there is a clear superior-subordinate equation between two people. It reveals an "I know everything" attitude and is used mainly by people who are experts or influencers in their field. The gesture is most common when people in positions of power are communicating instructions or offering advice.

There are two primary versions of the steepling hands' gesture. The raised steeple is when the person is trying to convey his stand or ideas on an issue. The lowered steeple, on the other hand, is when the steepler is listening to a person.

Rubbing Palms Together

Observe how entertainers, magicians, and master of ceremonies often rub their palms together while addressing their audience. Think about the salesperson who gleefully explains the benefits of his products while rubbing his palms. Rubbing palms is often a sign of excitement, enthusiasm, and expectancy. It's akin to the delight of a child waiting for his Christmas presents.

Rubbing palms is a sign that the person thinks something good is in store for him or you. For example, you want to buy a car and the salesperson shows you the model that he thinks best fits your needs. After describing all the features in detail, he says, "This is the right car for you!" by rubbing his palms together.

He is subconsciously signaling that he expects the car to be beneficial for you. When the palm rubbing movement is fast, it signifies a positive feeling. Similarly, if a person is rubbing his palms slowly, it may be a sign of manipulation, deceit, or devious intentions. The person is more likely focusing on their benefits at your cost.

Gripping Hands

Have you noticed the British royal family members? They walk with their head and chin held up. One palm is often gripping over the other behind their back. This gesture is used by several people in positions of authority. It reinforces a power equation between a superior and subordinate.

Holding hands behind the back is a sign of confidence, power, and authority. It is an act of making yourself vulnerable by exposing your pelvic region and stomach. The act almost always signifies fearlessness and confidence to take on the world.

Similarly, clenched fists denote firmness of resolution. Think of an athlete preparing himself ahead of a crucial game. It can communicate a high sense of unyieldingness, like a more aggressive version of face down palms. Tucking your thumb in signifies intense discomfort and anxiousness.

Hands in the Pocket

Hands in the pocket indicate a sense of unwillingness, reluctance, and lack of trust. When a person's hands are placed in their pockets, you need to work doubly hard to gain their interest or trust. There has to be an effort to eliminate their doubts and get them to open up to the idea. This can be used by you brilliantly to subconsciously get your point across to people, especially when it comes to forging beneficial relationships and influencing people.

Hand on the Heart

The hand on your heart gesture communicates a deep-seated need to be accepted or trusted. It reveals an individual's desire to be believed by others. It is used for conveying sincerity, though it may not necessarily be a sign of honesty. It doesn't say, "I am speaking the truth." Rather, it says, "I may or may not be speaking the truth but I desperately want you to believe what I am saying." The person may be trying to communicate that whatever they are saying is coming directly from the heart, but that may just be something they are doing to make you believe they are speaking the truth.

Chapter Five:
Analyzing Leg Movements

Leg movements have been synonymous with a human being's tendency to make fight or flight choices. In a nutshell, the legs and feet often involuntarily react to external circumstances without being guided by the conscious mind.

In times of crisis, our brains are wired to freeze or run for cover. These are sublime responses marked by natural instincts. So how do you decipher a person's thoughts, feelings, and emotions through their leg and feet movement? Here are some power packed clues and their closest interpretations.

When a person's feet are pointed in your direction while talking, there is a decent chance they like you. They may be keenly interested in what you are saying or even in agreement with your idea. On the contrary, if the feet are pointed away from you, he or she may wish to be somewhere else. They are on a deeper level attempting to walk away from the conversation. The person may not be comfortable being where they are.

Use this analysis to your advantage. If you see someone turning their feet in the opposite direction, make your point fast and go. The person may not be too keen on hearing from you. Stop dragging the conversation any further. On the contrary, when their feet are pointed in your direction, go on with what you are saying because the other person is accepting your ideas with a receptive mind.

Crossing legs is another common body language posture that can have multiple connotations. Crossing legs is a common sign of the person being rigid or non-receptive to ideas. The person may not be to open to your ideas or trust you. They may also be suspicious or in disagreement with your views. It is a subconscious signal of closing yourself to the other person.

They are mentally shutting themselves off from what you are saying. The topic of conversation is something about which they may hold a closed-minded opinion. Bottom line – the person may not agree or accept what you are presenting. If you want to persuade a person or get them to think/act in a certain way, first get them to open up their body language by changing the topic if their legs and arms are crossed. Once they are more comfortable with the new topic and uncross their hands and legs, go back to the original topic. Make the subconsciously receptive by getting them to change their body language. Once they are subconsciously receptive to what you are saying through their body language, they are likelier to agree to or accept your view.

There can be another meaning to crossing legs. It can be a sign of submissiveness or trying to win points. It can also point to low self-esteem, lack of confidence, or shyness. Again, for all you know, the person may want to pee really badly or are cold. Hence, they are crossing their legs while sitting. Look for other clues to validate your initial reading.

Notice how certain people stand with their legs apart, feet firmly on the ground. This means the person is very certain about what they are saying or doing. Other than confidence, it can also be an indication of dominance. They enjoy being in control of a conversation. This posture is observed in people of authority when they are giving instructions to their subordinates or reprimanding them.

The idea seems to be that they are the boss, and there's no challenging their ground. It can be an intimidating or authoritative gesture depending on the context. Men almost always stand in this position while approaching women they desire.

It simply reveals that they are self-assured and relentless, and nothing deters them. Lawyers also use a lot of feet on the ground posture in the courtroom to demonstrate the firmness and validity of their argument.

Foot tapping is common when people are restless, bored, or disinterested. It can also be a sign of anxiety, stress, and impatience. If someone is tapping their feet while you are speaking, it is a near clear indication that they are least bothered by what you are saying.

Tapping their foot on the ground allows people to get rid of the excess in-built energy that arises from either boredom or stress. They either lack interest or do not have enough conviction in your arguments or ideas.

It may be time to move on to another topic or change the approach. Foot tapping can occur in several forms such as tapping one foot above the other or moving it back and forth. However, at the root of it, it is related to boredom or stress.

Carefully take note of how a person stands when you are speed reading people. If an individual's legs are positioned to be parallel to their shoulders, they may be conveying dominance or even aggression. This is especially noticeable when a person is trying to make a presentation. Similarly, if a person is sitting with their ankles crossed and tucked beneath the chair, they are trying to hide their stress or anxiety.

Similarly, if a date or someone you desire is sitting with their legs held together, they are guarding themselves or may be uncomfortable with you. Legs kept neutral or in a balanced position reveal that the individual is more relaxed and prepared for anything that is about to come up. They aren't being cautious because they are confident, they can tackle anything. If the legs are placed in front of the person, he or she is being extra guarded and cautious.

Generally, people who are attracted to you will lean in your direction while speaking. Their legs and toes will be pointed in your direction. This will be accompanied by palms up sign that suggests openness.

People's movements while walking can reveal plenty of things about their character. Walking is only partly determined by intent; much of it has to do with our habit or personality. A person who generally walk fast (not occasionally since a one-off case may mean they are in a hurry) is an action-oriented and proactive individual who likes to have things done. Similarly, a habitual slow walker is someone who is a procrastinator, lazy, and low in ambition.

Chapter Six:
Using Verbal Clues To Read People Like a Pro

Verbal communication is everything that is conveyed through written and spoken language. On the face of it, it may seem easier to decipher than non-verbal communication, however, people are also experts at faking what they say, so its interpretation becomes slightly tricky and more meaningful only when combined with non-verbal communication.

Sometimes, relying only on non-verbal clues can be tricky, and you will need verbal clues to complement the non-verbal clues for gaining a better understanding of someone's exact motives, behavior, or personality. Imagine if you saw a person imitating a bird's flapping movement without knowing the setting or context. How would you interpret it?

The person could be playing some game, he could also be demonstrating the movement of birds to someone, he could be drying himself, or he may be living in an altered state of mind, where he thinks he's a bird.

There are innumerable interpretations of a person's behavior and movements, which is why you cannot solely rely on non-verbal clues or body language for a comprehensive interpretation of a person's behavior or personality. You also need to probe further and watch out for verbal clues that reveal more about their motives, behavior, and personality.

For instance, a person may not be feeling too positive or upbeat but may simply say they're not too bad. In this scenario, it is important to watch out for both verbal and non-verbal clues. Their words and the manner in which those words are uttered may point to the fact that they are in fact not too good.

In the above example, if the person says "not too bad," it can be interpreted as they aren't too good either. Of course, the person's regular verbiage and culture will determine how they usually speak, but their selection of words can reveal a lot about how they are feeling.

Let us consider another example. You open a nice new specialty restaurant in the heart of the city and have a steady stream of diners pouring in to try out the new dishes. Since the venture is still in its initial stages, you're eager to obtain feedback from your new customers to work upon the areas that need improvement.

You head to a family who has just finished eating their food for their feedback. The woman promptly says, "The soup was good." How would you interpret this? It can mean the soup was exceptionally good. However, there are higher chances that it means that nothing else was noteworthy except the soup.

When you learn to watch out for verbal cues, you're training yourself to read between the lines. People will often not spell out everything. They'll expect you to read their thoughts and feelings based on subtle verbal clues. For instance, don't we all hold a small grudge against people who say, you're looking good today. And we're doing the internal eye roll emoji thinking, don't I look good every day, why just today? Some positive souls will interpret it as this means I am looking exceptionally good today.

There are plenty of hidden clues in what people say and you just have to listen and watch keenly to comprehend the right meaning.

Excessive Talking

Talking too much can be both a sign of authority and a sign of trying to evade the real issue. It becomes all the more conspicuous when the conversation is peppered with a lot of fillers (aaaa, umm, hmm), silences, and repetitions.

People who are trying to hide something or deflecting from the real issue aren't generally very concise in their verbal communication pattern. They try to buy time by hammering the same point repetitively using different words and phrases.

Confident people in positions of authority or leadership seldom talk fast or in an incomprehensible, rambling manner. They spread out their words, their tone is more even, and speak in a clear, audible, and coherent manner.

Similarly, people who are more self-assured, honest, and open will convey things in a more concise, crisp, and unambiguous manner. They may not always use the right words (dependent on language abilities), however, they'll communicate in a more coherent and synchronized manner. Their sentences are less peppered with gap fillers and ambiguous words and phrases that are more open to interpretation.

Verbal Modeling

It is human nature to be drawn to people who are similar to us. We naturally talk to people who share the same interests as us, come from a similar cultural background, possess the same attitude as us, and even speak like us.

Therefore, people who are constantly trying to match your words and talking speed may be eagerly looking to be accepted by you or please you. Doesn't this happen during job interviews?

Sometimes, the interviewer is talking too fast, and the interviewee in his attempt to please the interviewer picks up the same speed or ends up choosing the same words and phrases subconsciously. This is referred to as mirroring in psychological lingo. You are simply mirroring the other person's words, actions, and attitude to impress them or demonstrate that "you're just one of them."

Listening and Acknowledging

A person who is keenly listening to you, cares about you, or is interested in listening to you will almost always throw in verbal acknowledgements in the form of "yes", "yeah", "I understand how you feel", "wow", "sure", "really", etc.

These verbal interjections and acknowledgments communicate that the person has heard you out and understood what you're trying to convey. People who are disinterested or don't care about what you're trying to convey will be less likely to come up with acknowledgment words and phrases during the process of the conversation. Beware if the acknowledgments are too frequent or over the top (if this isn't the person's usual baseline personality), it can be more contrived or fake.

Para-Verbal Cues

Since we've already discussed in the chapter, how there are can be abundant scope for misinterpretation while deciphering verbal clues, para-verbal clues (similar to non-verbal clues) help in adding more authenticity to our analysis.

Para-verbal clues comprise everything from tone to pause between phrases to the speed of one's speech to the volume in which a person speaks.

Fast paced speeches can reveal a more deceptive, disorganized, and uncertain demeanor, which is highlighted by ambiguous words and phrases. An evenly tempered speed can be an indication of self-assuredness, assertiveness, and balance. This person knows exactly what he wants, and is confident and comfortable expressing himself.

Similarly, a high voice volume can indicate authority or leadership. The person is trying to convey that he is in charge of the situation or trying to persuade people to accept his point of view or demanding attention.

There are several other verbal cues you need to watch out for while reading people. For instance, some expressions or sounds are used to complement words to make the message even more effective. Sometimes, the message is too intense to be conveyed only with the help of words, which means you need to watch out for sounds like screaming, laughing, sighing, and moaning to interpret the message accurately.

Word Signals

Notice how people are almost always dropping clues through their words. For instance, imagine a person has just stated that he's won another award. When you pay close attention to the choice of words, you'll realize that the person is trying to convey that he's won an award or several awards prior to this. He wants to ensure that people know he has done well previously too, thus boosting his image.

This person may be the kind who is constantly seeking validation, appreciation, and adulation from others to boost his self-esteem. He is likelier to be exploited using flattery and ego boosting praises.

Assume you are the owner of a fancy restaurant that serves diners multi-course meals. Your servers introduce each course along the way while offering detailed information about the preparations in each course.

To hand over the check to the group of diners, you discreetly walk up to the assumed leader of the group or the person paying the check and ask him or her, "Hope you enjoyed your meal sir or madam?" Pat comes the reply, "the soup was good."

Now, this simple, seemingly harmless statement can give you plenty of feedback about your food. If you read between the lines, it can mean the rest of the food was average or not worth it. Apart from the soup, everything else was ordinary.

Similarly, aren't we all offended when someone says, "You look good today." We are instantly on guard, "What you do mean today, don't I look good every day?" To this, the person will sheepishly retort, "No. I meant you look exceptionally good today."

We convey a lot through our choice of words, and even what we leave unsaid. Just like eyes are believed to be the windows to one's soul, words are a stairway to our mind.

Words are a reflection of our thoughts, and the nearest you can get to understand a person's inner thoughts, feelings, and emotions is by tuning in to the words they use while speaking and/or writing.

Word clues are important determinants of a person's behavior or personality, along with offering an insight into their thoughts and feelings. Of course, they aren't the only determinants of a person's personality but can be one of the aspects offering insights into a person's behavior.

The most effective way to go about it is probably deriving working hypotheses from the words people use, followed by testing it by using supplementary information sourced from other means. You are using additional information for corroborating the hypotheses.

The human brain is exceptionally efficient. While thinking, we fundamentally use nouns and verbs. Similarly, while transforming thoughts into written or spoken form, we resort mainly to using adjectives and adverbs. These words are a solid indication of our personality, feelings, and thoughts.

Take, for instance, the structure of a basic sentence. Say, "I ran." I is the subject and ran is a verb. Now, any words that are added to a simple sentence structure to build upon the noun or verb can offer solid clues about an individual's personality or behavior.

Here are some of the most commonly used words and terms and how they offer amazing insights into an individual's personality.

"I bagged another honor." Another here can convey that the speaker or writer already has a series of honors to his or her credit. He or she hasn't stated that already but it is clear through his or her choice of words.

The person may possess a deep sense of self-importance and may never miss an opportunity to let others know about his or her ingenuity. They may be conscious of their self- image and may need constant validation. These are the kind of people who are most vulnerable to flattery and ego-feeding comments.

Pronoun usage can effectively reveal an individual's personality. When you say "I don't really think I subscribe to that" instead of "I don't subscribe to that", it demonstrates self-focus. Even when simple questions like, "How is the weather there" are posed, self-focused people tend to respond with "I think it's cloudy and rainy."

If you wouldn't read this book, you'd probably brush off the "I think" as an insignificant add-on. However, it can be loaded with meaning. It reveals inward than outward focus.

People with emotional issues tend to use it more often than emotionally balanced individuals. They are people who struggle with self- esteem issues and consider themselves to be in lower positions who use "I" more often.

Similarly, an individual who is not speaking the truth tends to resort to more of "we" usage. There is a greater tendency to accept the blame and say "I" or "me." They tend to use more of "we."

These folks tend to eliminate speaking in the first-person completely. For example, instead of saying, "I haven't hidden your laptop," they will say "this isn't something an honest individual will do."

People with honesty and integrity tend to use words such as none or never more often. One of the best ways to develop an understanding of people's characters through their words is by pouring over court testimony transcripts. They can be extremely telling!

People who are telling the truth are likelier to use first person pronouns like "I." They will also use more specific words such as "except." This clearly reveals that they distinguish what they actually did and didn't do. Dishonest people, on the other hand, are not subconsciously equipped to deal with these complicated constructions.

Another important aspect that can reveal a lot about a person's beliefs and requirements are his jokes. Of course, you cannot analyze standalone jokes or isolated phrases. Again, like I always say, you'll have to watch out for other clues too. Generally, people's jokes not just reveal their sense of humor, but also a great deal about their personalities.

However, if a child jokingly says to the server, "I want to eat a dish that costs half a million dollars" you can't but help decode that he or she probably comes from a family that places great importance on money or financial security or he has been deprived on a financially stable environment.

Have you noticed how people repeat certain words or words that have similar meanings? For example, "his message was really powerful", "this book has a strong lesson" or "I don't possess the strength to run."

It may appear like the three statements may not be related. However, there is a very clear pattern when it comes to using the word powerful and it's synonymous.

Our choice of words isn't sporadic. It is driven or channelized by our basic needs, problems and concerns. The person who uses these words is more focused on strength or power.

He or she may be a person who yearns to be strong or powerful but is bogged down by feelings of weakness or inadequacy. They may want to gain more power or become stronger. Again, very revealing!

People can also be read and analyzed by their social media posts. A majority of what people like, write, and share on social media is a direct reflection of their personality and/or beliefs. You can gather a whole of social footprint/data to analyze people over a period of time.

However, you need a large number of posts to come to a near accurate conclusion about a person's behavior or personality. Picking up random, few, and far between posts may not be very effective because people's moods can frequently change. Sometimes, we write or share posts under the influence of temporary emotions.

Also, you need to link various posts for finding a common, underlying thread between all posts. A majority of the times, you'll find a clear theme highlighted in all posts that point to a specific behavior pattern.

For instance, people who lack self-esteem, yearn to be accepted, and desperately want to fit in may not shy away from showing off or underplaying their acquisitions and accomplishments.

A majority of an individual's social media posts point to a single direction, which makes it easier to decode their personality.

Even the pictures, memes, and videos a person share is important from the perspective of understanding his or her personality through social media. Would you really share something that is against your inherent personality or beliefs?

People share things that are congruent with their beliefs because they seek validation for what they believe in. The need to be accepted and to seek approval from others is socially wired in humans. People post specific posts on social media to gain support or validation from their social circle.

Is there a particular word that is being used frequently in an individual's post? We've seen how certain words people used can convey their hidden desires, core beliefs, and subconscious psychological motives.

For instance, if someone is constantly using words such as, "achieve, wealth, success, strive, dreams, objectives", the person may be ambitious or goal-oriented. It reveals your inner psychological objectives.

Similarly, if the individual is joking about money or the amount of money a famous personality makes or a brand new expensive car, you can identify a clear desire to make lots of money. They may make jokes about rich people or people's spending habits. There will be a clear and easily identifiable pattern.

Do the person's words match their pictures? For instance, if the person is using words such as "self-reliant", "rule my own life", "independent", etc. and have a lot of selfies or solo pictures on their page, you can conclude they are almost always self-reliant or on their own.

You can also establish someone's baseline by asking questions like, "How are you doing today Sally?" You're actually setting a platform for asking more questions. The clues hidden in their answers can establish a clear baseline.

This method is generally used by salespersons for establishing the baseline of their potential customers. They will start by asking their potential buyers how they've been doing or how their day went and will open the conversation up for more detailed probing and discussion.

The trick to establishing a person's baseline through words is by asking open-ended questions. They will give you insights into how the person is thinking and feeling. Use the above tips to read their words carefully, before coming to a conclusion.

Alright, so we aren't all trained FBI personnel who can analyze potential criminals through their verbal and non-verbal clues. However, there are still plenty of ways in which you can decode a person's thoughts and behavior.

An important part of analyzing people through their verbal communication is to pay close attention to the words they emphasize while talking.

For instance, if your manager says, "I am firm about my decision to scrap this project." His emphasis is on firm, which means there is no way he is going to change his decision.
His choice of words and emphasis indicates that he's pretty damn sure not giving in to anything. The words we use and emphasize on are clear indicators of our thoughts, emotions, and feelings.

Our choice of words is filled with meaning. Contrary to what believe, we don't use words very consciously. They are guided more by the thoughts and feelings held in our subconscious mind. Words people use conveys a lot about their personality.

If someone is constantly emphasizing on the word "hard-work", they may most likely be more driven by challenges or their goals. They may be concerned with fulfilling long-term goals than short-term pleasures. It may be an indicator of a person who is reliable, resolute, and dependable when it comes to completing given tasks. Similarly, the manner in which we elevate or lower out pitch can be a reliable indicator.

Lack of Sync between Verbal and Non Verbal Signals

People can say anything they want and they often lie through their teeth because they get away with deception. However, when you spot incongruence in a person's words and body language or expressions, you know something is amiss. For instance, someone is mentioning that they are really fond of someone, and while saying it, they are almost involuntarily shaking their head.

Notice how people sometimes say something makes them extremely happy, yet while saying it, their expression is painfully somber. This can be revealing. However, don't jump to any conclusion until you are able to gather more information.

Practice your skills by watching chat shows or talks shows by turning the volume down. Try to guess what these people are saying simply by observing their expressions, gestures, and posture. When you're done writing what you think they are saying, watch again. This time, turn up the volume and check if their words were congruent to their expressions or body language.

Pay Attention to the Emphasized Word

You may not be a trained FBI agent, but there are still lots of sneaky tricks and clever strategies that can be used to read people accurately. One of the most important verbal communication cues is the word a person emphasizes on while speaking. This reveals a lot about what is important to him along with his choice of words.

For example, if your supervisor says, I've decided to go ahead with this idea and emphasizes on "decided", there's little anyone can do to change his mind. He's conveying he has already made up his mind, and that there's no further scope for communication. Words reflect our thoughts and feelings.

The words we use are loaded with meaning, which consciously or subconsciously ends up revealing plenty of underlying emotions. Similarly, the words a person uses can communicate a lot about his personality. It is an indication of a personality that's not impulsive, more thoughtful, and analytical. Look out for words people use (especially action words) while talking to you. It will tell you more than people think they are giving away.

If someone constantly emphasizes on the word "hard" in saying I worked "hard" to accomplish this or it is "hard work", they are most likely goal-oriented folks who love a good challenge and do not like to be given things on a platter. It also suggests that the person is capable of delaying gratification or holding off pleasure until they achieve the results they are after.

If an employee is constantly using the term "hard work" (yes I know they all do and they lie too in which case you have to look for a combination of clues to spot inconsistency in their verbal and non-verbal clues), he may be a more goal-oriented and diligent employee, who doesn't shy away from taking up challenges or big responsibilities. He may possess the required determination to finish the given the assigned tasks, and can be dependable.

However, you have to be careful in situations like interviews, where people are aware that their personality, body language, confidence, etc. are being assessed in a more controlled and closed environment. This gives them the ability to manipulate the actions and body language to create the intended impression. However, if you have a trained eye and some practice, you'll quickly detect any inconsistencies.

Chapter Seven:
FBI Style Strategies for Reading People Instantly

Now that you've gained some expertise in analyzing people's behavior, let's sweeten the deal and give you even more amazing tips and tricks to read people like books.

Here are amazing strategies that will give you insights into what people are thinking and feeling to help you understand them better and develop even stronger interpersonal relationships.

1. Even seemingly innocuous questions such as "How are you today?" may be an attempt to establish your baseline, thus setting the stage for further probing and inquires. This technique is typically used by salesman and business associates. If you're trying to establish someone's baseline, gently probe them about how their day was or how they are doing today. It opens the gates for further discussion, probing, and negotiation.

Ask more open-ended questions if you want to set an initial baseline for interpreting people.

2. Children are brilliant subjects to practice on when it comes to detecting liars. If you're looking for signs to spot a liar, simply observe what children do when they lie. Annie Duke, a renowned professional poker player and cognitive psychology doctoral student, suggested that kids are an excellent source to pick up cues about deception.

Adults pick up deception skills to bolster social interactions and personal relationships, which kids haven't mastered at that stage. Therefore, they are pathetic at lying. Every sign is clearly visible because they aren't yet adept in the art of lying. Therefore, observing clear signs of deception in them gives you the ability to spot the same signs in adults.

This, of course, comes with its own fine print. Some people will be better at lying than others. Those who have mastered the art of deception will obviously be well versed in hiding signs of untruth.

3. Former FBI agent Joe Navarro offered many effective tips on reading people in *Psychology Today,* one of which included avoid vague questions after establishing a baseline. A rambling individual is tough to interpret. Therefore, ask straightforward questions that have a direct answer, which makes it easier for the questioner to detect deception. Don't look or appear too intrusive. Simply throw a question and observe minus interruption.

4. Genuine smiles are easy to tell apart from contrived or exaggerated smiles. When a person is genuinely delighted to see you or by the conversation they're having with you, their smile reaches the eye. It also slightly crinkles one's skin to form crow feet. Smile is the single largest arsenal people use to hide their true feelings and thoughts.

If you want to tell whether a person is smiling genuinely, watch out for likely a deception in the absence of these signs.

Did you know that a genuine smile is called Duchenne smile? It is believed that a smile can never be faked however hard a person tries. Have you ever wondered why you or someone ends up looking so awkward in pictures? It may appear on the fact of it that we're smiling, but we're actually only pretending to smile. Since a genuine smile elevates your cheeks a bit, there are bound to be some crow feet, which bundles up just below the eyes. Body language experts say this is tough to fake.

You actually need to experience a happy or joyful emotion to be able to create that expression. When you're not comfortable from within or not experiencing genuinely happy emotions, the expressions just do not fall into place.

5. When someone nods excessively or in an exaggerated manner, it means he is simply conveying his anxiety about your opinion of him. The person is also likely to think that you aren't confident about their abilities.

6. Clues that convey discomfort, stress, and distress include a furrowing brow, clenching jaws, compression of lips, and tightening of facial muscles. Similarly, if someone is shutting their eyes for longer than a regular blink or clearing their throat, there's a high chance they're stalling. Leaning away from you or rubbing hands against their thighs or head is also a sign of high stress.

7. Our brains are by default hardwired to interpret power or authority with the volume of space occupied by someone. For instance, an erect posture with straightened shoulders conveys authority. It communicates that you are occupying the optimum available space.

On the other hand, slouching is occupying less space and presenting yourself in a more collapsing form, thus demonstrating reduced power. People who maintain a good posture automatically command respect on a subconscious level.

8. Avoid making assumptions. One of the best tips you can receive while analyzing people is not to make prior assumptions or have any sort of biases or prejudices.

Sometimes, we go to analyze people with a clear prejudice and think we've already found what we've been seeking. For example, if you assume (based on prejudices, etc.) that a person is angry, then all their actions and words will seem like there's a deeply hidden anger within them. You will find only what you are looking for.

For instance, if we go to a person's workplace assuming that he is totally disinterested in the job or dislikes it, we'll assume his concentration or lack of cheery approach as absolute disinterest in the job. He may be strictly trying to focus on his job as opposed to hating it. Not everyone grins and laughs when they are enjoying their work. Sometimes, they are just involved in performing it more diligently.
Another important point is to avoid judging other people's personalities based on your own. For instance, in the above scenario, if you truly love your job, you'd have a more positive, grinning, and happy expression as opposed to a more somber look. However, not everyone shares your unique traits, behavior, attitude, beliefs, and values.

9. Stand opposite a mirror to observe your own body language. Give yourself various scenarios (party, informal outing with friends, a business presentation) and start talking like you would in these settings.

Being aware and conscious of your own body language in varied settings will help you identify patterns on other's body language too. Not just the mirror, the next time you find yourself at a negation table or first date, try to be more aware of your body language and the impression you are trying to convey. This will help you decipher the other person's thoughts and emotions more effectively through their body language.

Observe your own body language without being self-conscious or judgmental. Look how your eyes light up when you are talking about someone you care for deeply, notice how your eyebrows crinkle when you are speaking to someone you don't really like or trust.

This will help you gain a better understanding of other people's thoughts and feelings.
Notice everything from your eye movements to gestures to posture. This will help you understand exactly what you need to watch out for while analyzing other people.

By tuning into your own underlying feelings and emotions, you will be able to judge other people's body language, words, and actions more accurately.

10. Identify behavior patterns. Take for instance you're flying in an aircraft and a particular cabin crew member looks really pissed off while talking to a passenger seated near you. Now, you can quickly jump to the conclusion that he/she has an inherently arrogant, impatient, and hostile personality.

However, he/she may have just fought with his/her partner before boarding the aircraft, and may still be carrying the anger within him/her. You really can't tell if it's the former or later until you observe a clear or repetitive pattern.

Does she look particularly annoyed when passengers ask for something? Well, then you've spotted a pattern. If not, you're just being plain unfair in judging him/her based on a single isolated pattern that originated due to another external situation (argument with her partner). Looking for patterns helps you analyze people more objectively and accurately.

Look out for microexpressions. If you observe people closely, you'll notice that their real thoughts or feelings (and not what they're trying to deceptively convey) will be flashed on their face in the form of microexpressions.

Sometimes, while trying to come across as consoling, they'll quickly let off a smirk that can last 1/15th of a second. This is because their thoughts and expressions are syncing involuntarily for a moment.

Next time you're traveling by aircraft, notice how flight attendants smile with the help of their mouth but their eyes are blank, and the eyebrows are in a positioned in a scowl when you ask for more drink.

The truth almost always slips out in the form of these tiny expressions or microexpressions. While it isn't difficult to fake body language, look out for the not so subliminal cues, which are a clear giveaway. It's pretty much like shooting stars, you've got to see it fast before it disappears.

11. Notice people's walk. The way a person walks can reveal a lot about him. People who are constantly shuffling along demonstrate a clear lack of coherence of flow in things they take up.

Similarly, people walking with their head bowed reveal a lack of self-confidence or self-esteem. If you do observe one of your employees walking with their head down, you may want to help build the person's spirit. Appreciate him more in public and give him tasks that demonstrate your faith in him. Approach him by asking him open-ended questions during meetings to get him to talk more and bounce ideas off people.

When people try to manage their body language by misleading others, they concentrate on their postures, facial expressions, gestures, and postures. Since their leg's movements are more unrehearsed, this is where you're most likely to find deception. When in stress and duress, they will display signs of nervousness, fear, and anxiety with their legs.

If you watch closely, their feet will fidget, shift, and wrap around each other to make increased movements. The feet will involuntarily stretch, kick, and curl their feet to eliminate tension.

Research has revealed that people readers will enjoy higher success analyzing a person's emotional state just by observing his/her body. Even though you may not be aware of it until now, you've been intuitively responding to leg and foot gestures all the while.

12. Power play with voice. Much as people like to believe, the most powerful or commanding person is not the one at the helm of the table. It is the person with a confident, firm, and strong voice. Confidence denotes power.

At any conference table or business lunch, the most powerful and influential/persuasive individual is the one who has a confident and commanding voice, and huge smile (smiling is a sign of effortless confidence almost like the person is so good, he doesn't have to try too hard).

However, do not confuse a loud voice with a confident/ strong voice. Merely speaking loudly won't earn you respect if you sound shaky and confused.

When you're pitching an idea/product to a group of decision makers or people in general, watch out for people with the strongest and firmest voice. These are the people the leader may generally rely on for making decisions or these are the group influencers.

When you learn to observe and identify the strong voices, your chances of a positive outcome increase drastically.

People in power often keep their voice low, relaxed, and maximum pitch. They don't speak in a tone that elevates in the end, as if they are asking a question or sounding uncertain/doubtful about something or looking for approval. They will spell their opinion in a more statement like manner by employing a more authoritative tone that elevates in the middle of a sentence, only to drop down in the end.

Compare behavior. When you've noticed that someone is behaving particularly out of sync within a group of people or in a specific setting, observe whether they display the same behavior in other groups too. Also, if someone is acting slightly off the normal course with a person, try and gauge if they repeat the same actions with others too.

Continue to observe the person's actions in multiple settings to gain a comprehensive insight of his personality or behavior. Does the individual's expression or gestures change? Does his posture undergo a transformation? What about the voice and intonation? These clues help you know if the behavior you observed initially is a norm with them or simply an exception.

Chapter Eight:
Be the Ultimate Deception Spotting Pro

There are definite, telltale signs of deception because even though a person can control what he or she says, they cannot control their involuntary or subconsciously directed actions. Their neurological functions lead to certain physiological movements that aren't controlled. Spotting a liar is both challenging and simple. It becomes easy if you carefully look for the right clues and learn the art of probing (or knowing more about the person). Here are some typical deception clues that reveal a person is misleading, manipulating, or lying.

1. A habitual liar will almost always move physically away from a person upon being confronted. They will physically step back in a subconscious attempt to avoid confrontation or speaking the truth.

2. Deceptive people do not maintain continuous eye contact on being confronted. They have a more shifting gaze, contracted pupils, and finger on the lips while speaking. These are typical facial clues for liars. Their eye movements are more sporadic and rapid. There is no

pattern in the way their eyes dart from one direction to another.

3. Watch out, however, that you don't make sweeping judgments or accusations based on these signs. There can be other reasons causing it. As an interviewer, you may conclude that a person is lying when in fact he or she is plain nervous or stressed during the interview. To ascertain whether a person is telling the truth, simply ask the right open-ended questions. The more you get them to talk, the more clues and discrepancies to can spot in their words. Buy more time to establish if the person is indeed lying based on verbal as well as non-verbal clues.

Sometimes, people are just awkward, nervous, or shy by nature. Their lack of confidence shouldn't be confused with deception. Look to establish a clear baseline personality along with factors such as the person's values and cultural upbringing. Develop a keen observational eye that helps you call out deception almost accurately.

One of the tips I swear by is confronting and observing a person's reaction when I am 100 percent sure he or she is telling the truth. I keenly observe their voice tone, expressions, gestures, and posture. This helps you contrast their behavior when you are suspicious that they are lying. If you don't see more or less the same signs as to when they were speaking the truth, there's something wrong. Observe their mannerisms, statements, and voice tone.

Experienced behavioral analysts, people readers, and body language experts who have closely worked with investigation services with tell you that unmasking deception is easy when you establish the person's normal behavior. When you know how a person usually behaves, it is easy to call out abnormal or unusual behavior.
4. People who lie at times stand abnormally still. It is a commonly known fact that liars are often nervous and

fidgety. However, since liars are also aware of this fact, you also need to watch out for the opposite where the person is abnormally still to avoid giving any clues of nervousness. People who don't move or shift at all while talking should also be on your radar.

This can be traced back to our primitive neurological fight or flight syndrome when the body prepares itself for an impending confrontation. While speaking normally, our body naturally moves in a more sublime, relaxed, and subconscious manner. When a person displays a rigid, almost still position, it is a huge sign something is not right.

5. Pay careful attention to a person's voice when you are trying to determine whether they are speaking the truth. The person will not just start speaking faster than normal, but there will also be a very prominent tension in their voice. The pitch will become abnormally high and their tone with quaver ever so slightly. You've got to watch out for a stuttering, shaky, and stammering tone that clearly points to a lie if the person isn't nervous or stressed.

6. There is an excessive repetition of words and phrases. This happens because they are making an extra effort to convince the other person of their innocence. In their mind, they are subconsciously trying to validate the fact that they didn't do something and hence keep repeating it in the hope that the person will believe them. There is a tendency to use the same words or phrases over and over. It is also a trick to help them buy time for gathering their thoughts and reconstructing their version of events.

7. Deception is often characterized by faster breathing rate, speaking faster than normal, perspiration, a slight change in the complexion of the facial and neck zone, and speaking in a pitch that's higher than usual. Sometimes, the person will clear their throat more frequently than normal

in an attempt to buy time for reconstructing his or her version of events.

8. One of the most marked physiological signs of deceit is a quick change in the breathing pattern of an individual. When people lie to you, they start breathing rapidly. It is an involuntary action over which they have little control.

The breathing pattern changes and the shoulders are slightly elevated. The voice becomes shallower. The person will almost be panting or breathless because there are physiological changes in the body such as changes in blood flow and increased heart rate. The body witnesses specific changes when you are anxious or tense. This is exactly how lie detectors call out liars, based on rapid changes in their physiological functions.

9. A person changes his or her head position rapidly when they are lying. Liars often make sudden and rapid head movements while talking. The best thing to do in this scenario to find out more about the act is to throw them a direct question. The head is generally retracted, withdrawn, or jerks back. It is also bowed down at times. They will tilt their head to the side or keep it in a cocked position. This happens right before they respond to a confrontation question.

10. People who are not speaking the truth will give a lot of extra information. Liars tend to speak a lot and offer unwanted details. They will give plenty of information that isn't asked for and beat around the bush rather than coming straight to the point. They speak a lot in the hope that if they talk too much, people will buy their openness and believe them. They speak a lot to make it come across as transparency and openness, but if you are a trained people reader, you'll realize this isn't anything more than a cover-up attempt.

Lying is almost always associated with a big pause. It is a highly complex psychological and physiological process where your brain logically knows that you aren't telling the truth, but emotionally or psychologically you are trying to deny the truth, which makes it a very complicated process. The brain is processing the truth on one side, while the person is busy inventing another version of events to suppress the truth. This creates a fairly lengthy pause before replying, followed by a stalling attempt such as asking the other person, "Why are you asking me this?" rather than giving a straightforward and transparent response.

11. The toughest challenge for liars is to keep their hands and feet steady. They often struggle to keep their limbs in control, which is brilliant from an observer's point of view. When people's verbal communication is incongruent with their gesticulation, they aren't speaking the truth. When a person is telling the truth, their words and gestures will not have a mismatch. This happens mostly with the hand and feet. While liars insist they are telling the truth, their hands and feet move in a manner that isn't in sync with what they say.

12. People don't make eye contact when they are lying. However, again, the liar armed with this information will make an extra effort to maintain unflinching eye contact. This is a tactic for controlling and manipulating you. Deceptive people can also overcompensate by staring at people without blinking. When people are speaking the truth, their eye movements are more spread out relaxed. There isn't excessive staring or lack of eye contact. They will look people in the eyes but also occasionally shift their gaze in another direction. The eye blinking pattern will rapidly increase.

On the contrary, liars have an almost cold, calculated, and unshifting gaze to intimidate, control or manipulate people into believing them. The liar has most likely become hostile, angry, and defensive and is trying to turn it back to you. This is a sign of the liar's anger after being caught, and he or she is not attempting to give it back to you in a more aggressive and intimidating manner.

13. Liars will resort to touches for comforting themselves. There is predictably greater stress or anxiety when someone isn't speaking the truth. They are obviously scared of being caught or having their cover blown.

This leads them to often carry out self-comforting gestures such as rocking themselves, stroking or fidgeting their hair, twiddling with objects, hugging themselves, etc. These gestures become even more marked and dramatic when they are confronted. Watch for signs such as playing with their ring or looking preoccupied with something.

14. Pay close attention to someone's reaction when they are asked confrontational questions. Someone who is speaking the truth doesn't feel the need to justify themselves or over defend their stance. However, someone with a motive to over-defend themselves will launch into several defense mechanisms such as stalling, denying, offending the other person, or deflecting the truth.

A person who is speaking the truth will give details about the areas where people are expressing disbelief. The details will not be random, unlike people who are lying. They will address specifically those areas or offer details where they think people do not believe them. On the contrary, a person who is lying will keep repeating what they've already said rather than offering new details. When they give out too many details, they realize that there will be inconsistencies in facts. They will have to make more effort to mentally review everything they've said, which means they avoid saying more. They'll avoid coming up with new details and keep repeating the same things over and over again.

15. Have you ever observed how some people are constantly touching their nose while talking? They are more often than not lying. People tend to touch their nose frequently when they are lying because there is an adrenaline rush in the nose capillaries, leading to an itchy feeling on the nose. The person will touch his nose in an attempt to scratch his nose and cover his mouth to avoid blurting out the truth. Their mouth is tenser, while the lips are pressed, which leads to greater stress.

16. Microexpressions are clear giveaways of a person's deceit. The expressions are flashed across the face in a matter of seconds and you've got to possess a trained eye to spot them. Investigators will often spend hours trying to watch filmed tapes of potential criminals for telltale signs of deceit.

The footage is often slowed down to spot the exact expressions occurring in split seconds. When is the best time to spot these microexpressions of deceit? Exactly when the person has finished speaking. If they are lying, the mouth skews slightly and the eyes roll. This is an immediate giveaway that the person has not spoken the truth.

Since microexpressions flash on the face for split seconds, it is tough to fake it. While macro expressions are easy to manage or manipulate, these split second and involuntary physiological reactions are almost impossible to fake. Microexpressions reveal a person's innermost feelings and thoughts. Even if you aren't naturally intuitive or perceptive to these signs, it is fairly evident with some training.

Watch out for signs such as a person's eyebrows brows being pulled upwards to the middle of their forehead, leading to the appearance of short lines across the forehead.

17. Closely observe the person's eye movements to tell if they are speaking the truth. The direction in which a person's eyes go is a clear giveaway of whether they are recalling details or simply making something up. When left-handed people are trying to recall details, their eyes will move up and then towards the left, while the eyes of right-handed people will move to the right if they are making up a story. The reverse is also accurate for both left and right-handed people. Not just this, people also start rubbing their eyes rapidly when they are lying.

Pay careful attention to the person's eyelids. They tend to blink more than normal when they are in a denial mode. Liars don't accept that they are lying or are not in agreement with the person who has confronted them. By blinking continuously, they are trying to blank out or block the truth from their vision. People looking in a specific direction can help you determine the validity or veracity of their claims. You can easily pinpoint when people are lying by observing the direction of their eye movements.

18. Most liars tend to avoid exaggerated hand gestures in an attempt to avoid giving themselves up. They will avoid gestures such as pointing fingers, keeping an open palm, creating a triangle with fingertips, and other similar gestures. Observe their knuckles. Liars act motionless and grip objects almost until their knuckles turn pale. Watch out for excessive grooming gestures such as fiddling with the hair, adjusting their collar, playing with the cuff, and more.

19. Liars tend to give out impulsive or sudden emotional reactions. It is either because the person has practiced the

answer to these set of questions or randomly says something to fill up the silence. Another important verbal clue when you ask a straightforward question to the person, and he or she replies immediately without even thinking, there is a big chance that the person has rehearsed their reply. This is a clear indication of lies.

20. Let us look at typical verbal expressions of liars. They will not just repeat what they are saying but also resort to stalling for buying more time. They will ask you to repeat a question or use lots of fillers such as "the thing is that" or "what actually happened was" or "basically it is like this." They won't answer in a straightforward yes or no manner. Rather, they will come up with replies such as "It really depends on how you interpret x" or "how did you acquire this information?" They will counter question you in a bid to buy more time.

Another common verbal expression pattern among liars is that they will generally not use contractions of words. Instead of saying, "I didn't do something" they will tend to say, "I did not do something" to emphatically cover their tracks. There is also a tendency to speak in muddled statements that do not make much sense. Liars stop abruptly and pick up sentences randomly.

There is also a tendency to use sarcasm, one-liners, and humor to duck the subject. Other verbal signs of deception include words such as "to be honest" or "to tell you the truth." These reveal a deceptive mindset.

21. Many times, liars purposely slouch to give an illusion of being relaxed. They may go a step further and yawn or act bored simply to appear unperturbed or casual about the entire thing. This may be a huge cover-up attempt. Now, just because someone appears relaxed or unruffled, doesn't imply that they aren't lying. Sometimes, liars are not nervous or at least pretend not to be nervous.

22. Closely observe the throat of a person for deception clues. When a person is lying, their adrenaline secretion becomes high, thus leading to low saliva creation. There is a constant attempt to wet the throat by swallowing or gulping saliva. When the surge of salvia reduces, the person will most likely resort to gulping their throat.

23. If you actively want to observe signs of deceit when they aren't very prominent, simply stare hard at the person with a sense of disbelief (frown and wrinkles on the forehead). They will most likely feel uncomfortable with the stare. People who are speaking the truth will get angry or impatient. They will have their lips pursed together along with a tensed eyelid.

24. Stay patient and silent if you really want to know the truth. Don't give them any feedback about whether you believe them or not. By staying silent, you'll make the person feel uncomfortable. To cover up the sense of discomfort, they'll start resorting to conversation fillers. They will most likely embellish the conversation with details, giving themselves up in the process. Sometimes, people offer details that nail them without even being asked about it.

Just like you are analyzing the other person, the liar is trying to read you. They are trying to understand whether you've bought their story. If you don't reveal any signs of whether you trust them or not, the story will be unfolded by them. Be a great listener and practice the art of listening to people with interruption. This will help you gather many important details from a potential liar.

25. If a person's head is shaking in disagreement or opposition of what others are speaking, it is incongruence, which can be a telltale sign of deceit. For instance, a person may shake their head while saying he or she did or didn't do something. They may lie about doing something

but they are shaking their head, which means subconsciously they don't believe it to be true. Unless the person is a habitual, trained liar, it is impossible to control this incongruence.

Also, when a person is speaking the truth, they don't hesitate before nodding their head. The refusal and nodding take place at almost the same time, whereas when a person is lying, there is a slight delay between denial and the nod. The delay occurs because the mind takes some time to process the true and untrue version.

26. Projection. Liars are adept at using a technique called projection. When posed with a confrontation question, they respond with a counter question after an extended pause. The questions they pose will be more or less accusatory in nature. They will make you feel guilty for questioning them. The questions can be along the lines of, "Why were you snooping around my stuff?" or "You really think I am lying?"

27. Look at the shoulders. Sometimes, a person's shoulders close in when they are lying. There is a subconscious need to diminish themselves because they may believe they have done something wrong. They operate with a sense of vulnerability that their lie may be discovered, which causes them to hunch. The elbows generally come together and the person assumes a pose that makes them look smaller.

Chapter Nine:
Demystifying Personality Types

The study of personality is broad, varied, and evolving. Different schools of psychological study have come up with different theories about analyzing personality including dispositional (or trait-based study), biological, social learning, and psychodynamic.

Personality refers to a person's unique characteristics related to feeling, thinking, and behavior. It emphasizes predominantly on two areas – understanding differences between people with regards to specific characteristics and bringing together all characteristics to understand the person as a whole.

Let's take a look at some psychological personality types to help us gain a better understanding of people's baseline, which can then be used in combination with verbal and non-verbal cues to help us read them even more accurately.

Type A, B, C, and D Personalities

The Type A and Type B personality theory were first introduced by cardiologist duo Ray Rosenman and Meyer Friedman in the '50s.

Type A was known to be at a greater risk of coronary heart diseases than Type B since the former are known to be short-tempered, highly competitive, sensitive, proactive, multitasking, impatient, and always in a hurry. Type A personality people demonstrate an ambitious, hard-working, status-conscious, and aggressive disposition. They are always anxious to accomplish, which in turn leads to higher stress.

Type B, on the other hand, are known to be reflective, even-tempered, innovative, less competitive, low on stress, and unaffected by time constraints. If you're a classic Type B personality, you are moderately ambitious, live for the moment, and work more steadily.

Type B folks are social, procrastinating, creative, easy-going, modest, mild-mannered, and lead a more stress-free, laid-back life.

Later theories (that evolved to encompass even more personality types) found it constricting to divide all people into a Type A or Type B personality. Some people displayed characteristics predominantly from Type A but also displayed Type B traits. Thus, it became obsolete to classify people into two personality groups, which is why more personality types evolved.

A typical Type C individual has a fastidious eye for detail and is focused. They are inherently curious and are constantly trying to figure out things. There is a strong tendency to put other's needs before yours, and avoid being assertive or speaking up.

Typically, Type C will never mention straightaway if they like or dislike something. Over a period of time, this leads to resentment, stress, and depression. They take everything in life seriously, which makes them dependable workers. Possessing great analytic skills and intelligence, they just need to develop some assertiveness and learn to relax a bit.

Type D people have a more negative perspective of life and thrive in pessimism. Even a tiny event is enough to mess up their entire day. They tend to be more socially withdrawn and suffer from a deep-seated fear of being rejected, even when they enjoy being with people. They are at a higher risk of suffering from mental ailments since these folks predominantly lean towards melancholy and pessimism.

There is a greater tendency to suppress emotions, making them more prone to anxiety and depression. They expect the worst in any situation and do not share their feelings or emotions with people easily owing to the fear of rejection.

Trait Theory

The trait theory is primarily concerned with establishing the fundamental traits that provide a meaningful or coherent description of an individual's personality. It is also concerned with measuring these traits.

How does one draw a conclusion about an individual's personality based on the trait theory? He attempts to answer questions related to his feelings, thoughts, actions, and attitude. With the help of a personality inventory and rating scale, the individual's personality is determined. It is a combination of his responses and observation by the assessor.

Trained psychologists who observe these individuals rate them on a bunch of questions such as, how would you rate the individual's self-confidence? How would you rate the given subject's emotional balance?

Individuals are rated on a number of traits such as integrity, perseverance, sociability, dominance, etc., which in turn offers an analysis of the individual's personality.

Psychoanalytical Theory

This theory is dramatically diverse from the trait theory. While trait theory mainly relies on analyzing people based on what they've stated about themselves, psychoanalytic theory is an in-depth analysis of unique individual personalities.

Since the motivation is essentially more unconscious or subconscious, the analysis is believed to be more accurate. In the psychoanalytical theory, an individual's verbalization and behavior are considered to be a disguised manifestation of his most underlying subconscious/unconscious mind emotions.

The theory was first put forth by Sigmund Freud, when he compared a person's mind to an iceberg, where the surface makes up for our conscious experience, while the bigger masses under the water level represent our unconscious (comprising impulses, most primitive instincts, and deep passions that influence our actions and thoughts).

Freud's much-referenced psychoanalytic personality theory proposes that all human behavior is the direct result of interactions between the id, ego, and superego. This specific structural theory of personality focuses on the role of our unconscious/subconscious mind in modeling our behavior, actions, and personality.

Through the method of free association (dreams, experiences, childhood memories), Freud discussed analyzing people's most underlying feelings and emotions that determine their present attitude, behavior, and words.

Thus most behavior patterns and actions are traced back to the individual's early childhood experiences or memories that they aren't consciously aware of but are still lingering in their unconscious mind.

For instance, if a person displays more aggressive tendencies, it can be attributed to violent or aggressive experiences faced during their early childhood. If there is too much of a need to be accepted or please people, it can be traced back to being rejected by family members or friends.

Psychoanalysis is still widely used for helping people with issues such as depression, anxiety, panic attacks, obsessive behavior, aggression, anger issues, and more.

Social Learning Theory

This theory proposes that people pick up personalities or behavior patterns based on their learning from the immediate environment, and as such variations in behavior are a direct result of the diverse conditions in which we learn while growing up. Certain behavior patterns or personality traits are picked up through direct experiences.

For instance, an individual behaving in a particular manner may have been rewarded for it earlier, and hence is simply repeating what he learned through his direct experiences. For instance, someone constantly throwing tantrums and big on drama may have learned through early direct experiences that doing this helps them receive plenty of attention, which then becomes a behavior pattern.

However, responses can also be gained without direct experiences.

Since the human mind utilizes complex, symbolic codes to retain information based on observations, our behavior can also be a result of observing other's actions and consequences. Much of our observations and experiences are vicarious and complex. Reinforcement may not be needed for picking up or imbibing certain personality traits.

Carl Jung's Popular Personality Classification Theory

Noted psychologist Carl Jung classified an individual's behavior or personality based on their sociability — as introverts and extroverts.

Introverts are people who are predominantly shy, withdrawn, reticent, talk less, and are not comfortable in social settings. They tend to be more fixated on their ideas and are known to be sensible. It isn't easy to get them out of their shell and develop a rapport with everyone.

Extroverts are gregarious, outgoing, talkative, generous, courageous, and friendly. They are the classic "people's persons" who live more for the present than worry about their future. Their disposition is more happy go lucky and positive. Challenges do not shake them easily.

Later, psychologists added another type to Carl Jung's classic classification theory. They argued that only a handful of people display extreme introvert or extrovert tendencies. A majority of folks in fact possess qualities of both an introvert and extrovert. These people are referred to as ambiverts.

Ernst Kretschmer's Classification

German Kretschmer's classification theory attempted to connect an individual's physical characteristics with his personality, and certain mental ailments that they were most likely to suffer from.

He classified people into various types including Pyknic, Asthenic, Athletic, and Dysplastic. Pyknic types are folks who are short and round. They are said to display personality traits of an extrovert, known to be outgoing and gregarious.

The Asthenic type, on the other hand, are people who have a slim/slender appearance. They possess a predominantly introvert personality. The Athletic folks are people who have strong, well-built, and robust bodies, who display more aggressive, energetic, and ambivert traits.

The Dysplastic type essentially displays a disproportionate body and is not a part of any of three previously mentioned types. The disproportion is due to a hormonal imbalance, where a person's personality also reveals traces of imbalance.

Briggs Myers Type Indicator

There are several personality tests that individuals can take to have a psychological analysis of their most predominant personality. One of the most popular ones is the Myers-Briggs Type Indicator. It is a comprehensive and more reflective self-report that offers an analysis of people's personalities based on the manner in which they view the world and wield decisions.

The test was created by Katharine Cook Briggs and Isabel Briggs Myers (Katharine's daughter). It relies on Carl Jung's typological theory where he promised that there are four essential psychological functions experienced by humans — thinking, intuition, sensation, and feeling.

In every person, Jung stated, one of the four fundamental functions dominates over others. The MBTI focuses on naturally found differences between different types of people, with a fundamental assumption that every one of us possesses a clear preference in the manner through which we experience the world around us, and these differences, in turn, underline our needs, beliefs, values, interests, and motives.

According to this popular psychological personality test, there are about 16 varied types of personalities. The test consists of a bunch of questions, where the respondents' answers demonstrate their personality type. It also offers insights on how a particular personality is most suitable for success in different areas such as career, interpersonal relationships, etc.

Determining Personality Type

The Myers-Briggs personality type was a personality assessment system founded by mother-daughter duo Katharine Cook Briggs and Isabel Briggs Myers. It was invented with the objective of helping women find jobs that were most suitable for their personalities when World War II commenced. The idea was just like one side of the brain is dominant in each person, which makes them either left or right-handed, people are naturally inclined to think, feel and act in a specific manner. Each of us is in a sense comfortable of acting or behaving in a certain way, which determines our overall personality. Here are some tips for determining a person's personality type.

Is the person an introvert or extrovert?

The first reading parameter when it comes to reading an individual's personality should be if the person is an introvert or extrovert. This isn't as much about how social a person is as about how he/she tends to feel, think, and act. While solving a problem, do they reflect inward or look outward? Do they think more about themselves or other people? There's no right or wrong here. You are observing someone purely from the perspective of determining their personality, and no personality type is good or bad, right or wrong from a psycho-scientific angle.

People who look charged and energized around others or by social activities are likely extroverted by nature. They desire to be around other people and possibly have a large circle of acquaintances. Introverts, on the other hand, prefer spending time alone over socializing. These people generally have sharp minds and think rather than speak.

How does the person gather information?

While reading or analyzing people, pay close attention to how people gather information. Do they do it through a sensory experience or intuition? People who sense are focused on cold, hard facts, while those who feel operate on their hunches and gut feeling. Sensors don't depend on their gut feeling until it is backed by logic. They are more detail-oriented and mindful of their needs. Rather than relying on flashes of gut feelings or guesswork, they depend on observations of clean facts.

Intuitive folks, on the other hand, are more at home with feelings, abstract ideas, and theories. They are spontaneous, instinctive, and imaginative. They tend to live in a future that looks full of possibilities rather than merely existing in the present. Their thoughts are focused on patterns, links, and insight flashes. They have trouble living in the now. Have you seen people being so consumed and focused on future ideas that they forget to eat? These are most likely the intuitive people.

How does the person make decisions?

Determine how the person makes their decision after gathering information while determining their personality. Do they rely on other people's perspective in a bid to take a balanced and agreeable decision that makes everyone happy? This is typically the sign of a feeling person. Conversely, if they make decisions primarily by relying on logic and analyzing facts, their decision making demonstrates a thinking personality.

Feeling personality types are increasingly uncomfortable when confronted by conflict, while the thinking personality types accept it as a part of dealing with different types of people.

How does the person relate to the outside world?

The manner through which a person relates to the external world also establishes their personality type. Do they openly express their perceptions and judgments to other people? The judging type will offer people advice about how to make clear decisions and resolve matters.

They like to come up with practical solutions for problems and have a more problem resolution mindset. If someone likes to make plans, checklists, and complete things ahead of their given timeframe, they most likely belong to the judging type. Perceiving types like to share their observations with everyone around, keeping their options open before making up their mind. They tend to wait and watch until they make a decision or commit.

Getting a person to take the MBTI test is a great way to understand his or her personality. However, in the absence of this test, you can use the above pointers to determine their personality. The results may or may not be conclusive, but combined with other techniques mentioned in the book, you may succeed in reading people fairly accurately.

No one MBTI personality is greater than the other. The personality type test attempts to identify a person's natural tendencies, not abilities. Analyze people from the perspective of what they tend to be rather than how they should be or how you want them to be.

Here are the 16 fundamental personality types as defined by the Briggs-Myers Type Indicator.

1. INTJ
These folks are predominantly imaginative, creative, and strategic. They seem to have a ready plan for almost everything in life.

2. INTP
Innovative, analytical, logical, and curious, they rarely stop reasoning and questioning things. They are essentially inventive, intelligent, and creative.

3. ENTJ
These are your natural leaders. They are courageous, imaginative, unafraid of taking risks, bold, and extremely strong-willed. They rarely fail to find a way or in the absence of it, will create the way themselves.

4. ENTP
The quintessential debaters who can never resist a challenge that stimulates their intelligence, these folks are smart, argumentative, quick-witted, and curious.

5. INFJ
They are the unflinching idealists of the Briggs-Myers personality test. They are tireless, inspiring, calm, and mystical. The kind who let their actions speak louder than words.

6. INFP

These are the compassionate, kind, considerate, poetic, altruistic people, who never step back from contributing to a worthy cause.

7. ENFJ

These are people magnets, the charismatic, persuasive, and inspiring leaders who can hold their audience spellbound.

8. ENFP

They are creative, innovative, free-spirited, sociable, and always cheerful. These folks enjoy forging strong social and emotional bonds with others, and are often the proverbial "life of a party."

9. ISTJ

Their reliability and dependability can seldom be questioned when it comes to offering practical solutions. Fact-minded, high on integrity and analytical, the ISTJ personality types are accurate, patient, and responsible.

10. ISFJ

The ISFJ people are warm, devoted, protective, and forever ready to put their loved ones out of harm's way. They are kind, altruistic, enthusiastic, and generous. They possess well-evolved people and social skills.

11. ESTJ

They are known to be exceptionally good administrators with an unsurpassable ability to manage things, people, and situations.

12. ESFJ

Their caring and empathy quotient is above average, which tends to make them extremely popular and social. They are always ready to step in when people need help and make for exceptional sounding boards or counselors.

13. ISTP

These are the quintessential risk-takers, who don't shy away from wielding courageous and bold decisions. They are forever experimenting and trying to master varied skills.

14. ISFP

Flexible, adaptable, magnetic, charming, and artistic, they are always eager to explore new things and thrive of novel experiences.

15. ESTP

These are smart, enthusiastic, and perceptive people who live life of the edge. They are intelligent and make for energetic conversationalists.

16. ESFP

The ESFP personality type are enthusiastic, entertaining, spontaneous, and energetic people. Few other personality types are able to motivate and encourage others as much as these folks do. They have the most powerful aesthetic sense.

The Briggs Myers test is widely used in professional settings for leadership development, career selection, screening potential employees, promoting workforce, and team building.

Of course, like most other theories, it has earned its share of criticism for not being conclusive enough for generating "soft" results that cannot be completely applied in a business setting. However, despite the criticism, the test still offers a reasonable reading of a person's personality and can be a good value addition when it comes to reading/analyzing people. It can be more conclusive when conducted in combination with other psychological analysis techniques.

Certain types of personalities are more suitable for specific situations than other types. Knowing where others or yourself fall on the rating scale makes it easier for you (as a decision maker) to know where people are most likely to be comfortable.

For instance, knowing someone has a more introvert type personality will help you make the most of their preference of working in structured, tinier, quieter, and more organized settings. You'll quickly figure out that these people may not thrive while working in a team, and are more likely to maximize productivity by working alone.

Similarly, extroverts may flourish in huge, loud settings, surrounded by lots of people.
The Briggs Myers can offer a reasonably accurate (though not comprehensive) baseline for helping you analyze people using a bunch of other psychological and practical people reading techniques.

Bonus Chapter:
Examples of Reading People in Real-Life Scenarios

Now that we pretty much know the secrets of reading people, let's look at some real-life illustrative examples of how we can read people comprehensively and accurately.

Scenario One

Now, let's pick up another real-life scenario where you can apply people reading skills. You are a recruiter who is assigned the task of interviewing and selecting the best people for filling in a particular role.

This is another tricky one. If a candidate is blinking frequently, you may be likely to assume that he or she is extremely nervous. How can you be so sure that his or her lenses aren't causing discomfort? Again, avoid rushing to sweeping conclusions, and learn to identify underlying motives behind people's behavior.

Slouching is a big no-no. It can be an indicator of low self-confidence and respect for authority. The person may not be taking the interview process or job position seriously. The individual may not be an assertive and self-assured decision maker.

Similarly, I've come across plenty of people who sit on the edge of their seat. Now that's understandable when you are watching a thriller on television or the cinema, but not during job interviews. Sit in a comfortable and relaxed position.

If the candidate is sitting on the edge of the seat and leaning forward, that's a good sign. He or she is keenly tuned in to what you are speaking or wants you to hear exactly what they are saying. However, people intruding your personal space by placing themselves a little too close for comfort is again not a very positive sign.

Similarly, I also find a lot of candidates leaning behind during an interview. If you are the interviewer, this is another red flag. The person is may likely be defensive and may not accept responsibility or accountability for his or her actions.

Look at the candidate's shoulder movements carefully. If they are describing a certain experience with a lot of grandeur, but their shoulders are stiff or there's movement in a single shoulder, he or she may not be sure of what they are saying or maybe blatantly lying. Again, observe other clues before making judgments.

When a person is incessantly touching his or her face or fiddling with their hair, it can be discomforting or misleading. Similarly, continuously rubbing their neck is a sign of trying to calm themselves in a stressful situation. It can be an indication of stress due to lying too.
Crossing arms across the chest is a huge indicator of defensiveness and being closed to other's ideas. These

people may not be very secure and may appear distant or disconnected.

While it may be alright when someone is meeting a person for the first time or coming in contact with a stranger, the closed demeanor should slowly wear off during the course of the conversation. If it doesn't, the person isn't very open to your views or ideas.

While a majority of us take to fidgeting at one time or another, excessive fidgeting or playing with objects can be a huge sign of nervousness.

Some amount of anxiety and nervousness is acceptable in a job interview. However, if the person's role demands increased interaction with people and they are anxious while talking to you, that is not a very healthy sign.

Strong handshakes are a sign of confidence, assertiveness, mental strength, and determination. However, too firm of a handshake can also signify intimidation, control, dominance, or aggression.

If a candidate is shaking your hand too firmly, it may most likely be a sign of aggressiveness, arrogance, or trying to gain an upper hand in the conversation. This is also one area where you'll have to consider the cultural context as handshakes tend to vary from culture to culture. If handshakes are also accompanied by a genuine, warm smile, it is a good sign.

Eyes are believed to offer a glimpse into a person's soul. Direct and consistent eye contact is viewed as a sign of self-assuredness, positivity, integrity, and confidence. It is a sign of establishing trust, genuineness, and confidence. Someone who is constantly shifting their gaze and does not look into our eyes is hard to trust.

Having said that, analyzing a person's eye contact can be particularly challenging. Candidates who have a more piercing gaze can come across as intimidating, rude, and aggressive. They may even be looking down upon you.

Similarly, sometimes, not making eye contact may be a sign of nervousness and not deception. People also quickly shift their gaze when they are trying to recall or think about something.

Sometimes counterintuitively, people who lie may attempt to make even more eye contact to appear truthful.

Job aspirants are always under the scanner during interviews. They are aware that recruiters are closely watching and scrutinizing them. This, in no way, implies that body language is irrelevant or doesn't count.

However, a lot of the candidate's body language will depend based on your own body language as a recruiter. It's not a one-way street really. A lot of people's actions and reactions are directly dependent on your behavior.

A pleasant body language on your part will allow the candidate to demonstrate a more relaxed and open demeanor. Similarly, negative body language on your part leads to greater defensiveness and reservations by the candidate.

Avoid slouching or being fidgety. These signals can subconsciously get the candidate to act in a similar manner. As a recruiter or interviewer, you need to aware of your conscious as well as subconscious signals.

Also, a lot of times, people (especially job candidates) know that their body language and verbal clues will be assessed during the course of the interview. This makes it easier for them to fake it according to what they believe will create a positive impression.

However, as a trained observer of people, you'll instantly identify any behavioral inconsistencies. It's tough to fake everything at once. It is tough to fake a cluster of clues. Sometimes, their gestures and expressions may not match their words. Other times the tone of their voice and posture may be totally different. Trained people analyzers are able to spot these differences or inconsistencies.

Now, there are tons of verbal clues that will give you an insight into the person's thoughts and behavior. Candidates that speak with a clear voice, while maintaining a steady volume, intonation, and rhythm are likelier to be more balanced, dependable, and steady individuals who wield more rational decisions. Focus on their breath while they are speaking. Does it match the steadiness of their speech?

Talking fast or in a constantly wavering pattern can be a sign of nervousness, as well as deception. If there isn't clarity of speech, you'll have to look for other signals to establish that the person is indeed lying or unsure of his abilities. You may have to watch out for other signs such as tone, gestures, posture, expressions, and words.

Filler words such as "umm," "hmmm," etc. again point to lack of conviction and self-assuredness. These guys may be slow decision-makers or unsure of their abilities. People who use short, clear, and simple sentence are more in control of themselves and confident in their abilities.

Scenario Two

Let's assume you are out on a blind date. You don't know much about the person except what you've probably heard from a friend who has set you both up. How can you put together verbal and non-verbal clues to determine if they are indeed a perfect match for you?

Of course, it's not going to be easy when it comes to decoding a person's behavior through his or her body language on a date, because generally, people are in their best behavior when out on a date to charm their potential partner.

Develop a keen eye for observing verbal and non-verbal clues. How guarded is someone with his or her body language? On a first date, people aren't generally very open. They will most likely cross their limbs and maintain a considerable physical distance. Similarly, their palms will be inward facing.

However, as time passes or you move on to the second or third date, you'll begin to notice visible changes in the demeanor of the person. Rigid postures soon convert into more relaxed, warm, and inviting body language.

How do you feel the other person feel more comfortable and open in your presence? There is a powerful principle known as mirroring. This one simple technique can make you more likable and appealing to others.

Mirroring is nothing but following or mimicking a person's actions in a more subtle way. You can mimic the way a person is holding his or her glass, take a sip of the drink after he or she does, gesticulate like him or her, or even use the words he or she does. Be careful that it doesn't come across as if you are making fun of them or mocking them.

Mirroring works brilliantly on a subconscious level. The person is likelier to feel you are one among his or her own kind at a subconscious level when you mirror his or her actions. The persona will instantly connect with you and feel more at ease in your company.

Similarly, when someone else is mirroring you, he or she has most likely taken a liking for you and feels relaxed in your company. If you want a more tensed looking date to relax a bit, let your own guard down and display a more relaxed body language. He or she will receive the message on a subconscious level, and their body language will soon follow suit.

Throw your arms and palms open (or uncrossed). Offer a genuine smile (yes with the crow feet, crinkles, and all) and stay in close physical proximity to the person. Avoid moving away from the date during the course of your outing. Physical distance is a huge red flag for subconsciously distancing yourself from the person.

When you notice that a person's body language changes or becomes more rigid (or closed) when you are talking about something, quickly change the topic. They are probably not very comfortable or open to discussing the subject with you yet.

Scenario Three

This is going to be fun. Imagine walking to a party or a business networking event, where you do not know anyone except the host or organizer. Everyone here is a stranger who you have to make an attempt to get to know.

Just how will you do that? How will you determine or identify people who are open to your message and those that don't care a lark about what you are saying? Again, people reading skills to the rescue!

Let's start with my favorite, mirroring. We've discussed how mirroring is the best way to become more likable and appealing to another person. It is so effective because it's very primordial in its approach. When you lean against the wall exactly like someone you've just met at a party or hold your glass in a manner in which they do, you are making them more comfortable in your presence.

Similarly, if a person is constantly mirroring your actions (sipping on a drink right after you or copying your expressions), he or she may have taken a liking for you at the subconscious level. They may have felt you are just like them, and hence appear more relaxed and open in your company. Next time, try mirroring people's actions when you are getting to know them and observe the effect!

You introduce yourself and start talking to a stranger. Halfway through narrating incident or anecdote, you spot their raised eyebrows expression. What does that reveal? Well, most probably, he or she is having a hard time believing what you are saying or aren't convinced about your ideas. Raised eyebrows are almost always a sign of worry, disbelief, surprise, or fear.

Just try raising your eyebrows when you are in the middle of a warm, relaxed, and informal conversation with your best buddy. Is it possible? Pretty tough right? If the topic of conversation is an easy and relaxed one, it won't lead to nervousness or fear. If the topic you've initiated isn't rationally worrisome or fearful (say for instance you are telling a joke), then there's something else going on in the person's mind.

Have you ever noticed how when you are talking to or addressing a group, a couple of people in the group will be nodding excessively in an exaggerated manner? This simply means that they are highly anxious about what impression you have about them and are eager to be in your good books. These are people who are keen to make a favorable impression on you and are constantly insecure about you doubting their abilities.

Clenched jaws, furrowed brows, and tightened back and neck are indicators of huge stress. These clues reveal discomfort and lack of ease. The person may not be comfortable in your company or may be anxious about what you think about him or her. They may also be preoccupied with distress causing thoughts. The bottom line, like always, is to find a clear incongruence between what the person is saying and their body language.

One very important thing about analyzing people through body language is paying close attention to our own involuntary reactions as observers. Be cautious of the signals you are giving out while responding to others. Reactions and responses are at times channelized by conflicting motives.

Conclusion

Thank you for purchasing this book. I genuinely hope it has offered you several proven strategies, foolproof tips, and effective strategies for instantly reading people in various situations and settings of life, and made you the ultimate people analyzer.

Whether you are trying to gauge what a potential client is thinking during negotiations or if your hot new date is attracted to you or if you're hiring a suitable person, this book presents several practical techniques and wisdom nuggets to help you read people like books in all walks of life – even when they do not talk much!

The next step is to simply use this valuable resource by implementing these handy people reading pointers in your daily life. You aren't going to be an FBI type accurate people analyzer within a day. It will come with lots of observation, practice, and application. Learn to get into the habit of observing and analyzing people using these techniques in a variety of settings from supermarkets to airports to cafes, when you have some time at hand.

Finally, if you enjoyed reading the book, please take the time to share your thoughts by posting a review on Amazon. It'd be highly appreciated.

Here's to being a fantastic people analyzer, who can use the power of reading people's thoughts/feelings to transform lives and enjoy healthier relationships.

Other Books by Leonard Moore

Do you want to learn how to actually hypnotize people? Hypnosis isn't what most people think... Yes, hypnosis is real, but it isn't a magical way to make people do what you want. Neither it is a stage show, as some may make it out to be. This practice has been surrounded by mystery and false ideas for centuries, but the truth is that hypnosis is actually a very scientific process you can follow.

You see... hypnosis, the real hypnosis, is a natural phenomenon that can be harnessed to talk to somebody's subconscious mind and guide his decisions and actions, but most importantly it's also a skill that can be developed.

If you want to learn the real techniques to hypnotize other people, then this book is for you. In this book you'll learn how to hypnotize a person following a science based process that actually works. You'll learn everything about wording, hypnotic voice, scripts, body language, hypnotic induction and more.

You'll also discover the history of hypnosis, what's true, what's false and the different methods and procedures. This guide includes detailed instructions to help you build your own effective scripts to hypnotize other people, even if you've never done it before..

Inside Hypnosis you'll discover:
- An effective process you can follow to hypnotize a subject, keep him/her into trance and speak to his/her subconscious mind
- Common myths demystified (including "only people with low intelligence can be hypnotized" and "you can be hypnotized anytime/anywhere")
- Why we're all in trance very often without even noticing it and how you can take advantage of this to hypnotize others
- This small change in your voice can make a big difference the next time you hypnotize someone
- What are all the stages of an effective hypnosis session
- 5 things that can make a person more likely to fall in a hypnotic trance
- How to take advantage of a common natural phenomenon to successfully hypnotize people
- The #1 rule to follow when constructing an effective script to hypnotize people

- The history of hypnosis, from mysterious practice to stage show to scientific process
- Practical examples of what to say to induce hypnotic trance in your subject

And much, much more...

Even if you're starting from scratch, you'll learn how to perform an effective hypnosis session, including how to induce trance, how to talk to the subconscious mind and how to wake up your subjects.

"Hypnosis" by Leonard Moore is available on Amazon.

Made in the USA
Las Vegas, NV
15 September 2023

77614069R00066